PRAISE FOR *INK SPOTS*

"As a student of storytelling, I've been reading Brian McDonald's writings for a while now. I often find more wisdom in a single essay than in entire books about the art of narrative. By putting his essays together in this collection Brian offers a wealth of advice and reflections that will inspire and challenge anyone who wants to tell better stories."
– Andy Goodman, Author, *Storytelling as Best Practice*

"Brian's books and website are succinct, insightful resources for understanding not only the mechanics, but the purpose, of storytelling. I've recommended them so many times you'd think I was getting a piece of the action."
— Chris Warner, Senior Editor Dark Horse Comics/Books

"Listen to Brian, he has the unique ability to articulate what makes good writing."
— Al Higgins, Writer *News Radio, Malcolm in the Middle* and *Mike & Molly*

"Early on, Brian quotes the old adage, "It's not a sprint, it's a marathon," then proves it by turning a series of one-off essays into a complete philosophy of life behind the keyboard — and life. If you don't already have a mentor, here's one you'll love, in portable form."
— Steve Englehart, novelist and writer of classic versions of dozen of comics series such as *Batman* and *The Avengers*

"Brian McDonald taps into the universal truths and undercurrents of storytelling, and continually brings surprising discoveries to the surface."
— Derek Thompson, Story Artist at Pixar Animation Studios

"I use Brian McDonald's books in my classes because I'm a student of his work. All teachers are students all the time. Brian hasn't forgotten that he occupies both a seat in the classroom and the spot in front of the classroom."
— Shawn Wong Professor, Department of English University of Washington

"Brian's book is filled with insightful and useful gems for writers of any experience level. The only reason you'll want to put it down is to go start writing yourself."

— J. Elvis Weinstein, writer/producer *Freaks and Geeks, Mystery Science Theater 3000, Cinematic Titanic*

"Brian is that friend in movie storytelling that everyone deserves. He writes in clear, readily usable ways to improve your screenwriting. Like time-release story capsules they ignite and helped me over many movies and countless story bends. Give him a read, take a couple and repeat as needed."

— Ronnie del Carmen, story supervisor on *UP* and *Finding Nemo,* director and writer at Pixar Animation Studios.

"Critical, Insightful, philosophical, and inspirational. Brian McDonald's "Ink Spots" reads like a journal of his daily observations and thoughts about perceptions, mindsets, and the creative process. His stories recount wisdom from the giants of the past while giving us perspective as we head into the future. If you have ever aspired to create, you owe it to yourself to read *Ink Spots*."

— Sam Liu Director of *The Batman: Animated Series* and *All-Star Superman*

"Brian has shown me many new ways to look at stories, to analyze them and give me the analytical tools to even make some of my own. If you care enough about stories to want to know how they work their magic on us, read everything you possibly can by Brian McDonald."

— James S. Baker story artist, *Finding Nemo, Wall*E, UP*

"At the heart of the seemingly spontaneous often lies a web of intricate mechanics. There are few observers of this strange alchemy as clever and astute as Brian McDonald--a master of story dissection and character building alike. His keenest power, though, lies beyond the mere construction of solid storytelling: Brian has that rare gift known as 'good taste' that sets him apart from the simple technicians."

— Scott Morse story artist, *Ratatouille, Wall*E, Brave*

INK SPOTS

THE COLLECTED WRITINGS OF BRIAN MCDONALD
ON STORY STRUCTURE, FILMMAKING,
AND CRAFTSMANSHIP

BRIAN MCDONALD

TALKING DRUM

INK SPOTS

Library of Congress Control Number: 2016921320
Cataloging in Publication Data on file with Publisher

Paperback ISBN: 978-0-9985344-4-2
Kindle ISBN: 978-0-9985344-5-9
EPUB ISBN: 978-0-9985344-6-6

Publishing and Production: Concierge Marketing Inc., Omaha, Nebraska

Printed in the United States of America

10 9 8 7 6 5 4 3 2 1

For Aunt Patricia

FOREWORD

I HAVE A COFFEE CUP that Brian McDonald gave me. I love this cup.

On it is written one of his gems of story craft wisdom.

"Find that thing that your character would rather die than do and make them do it."

What wonderfully wicked advice!

Survival. Facing your fear.

According to Brian this is at the core of why we tell stories. They contain vital truths for living. Stories that help us become better human beings.

It reminds me that great stories are really crucibles of character.

The first time Brian and I worked together he had flown down to LA to help me with a story I was developing.

What neither of us knew was that he was going to have to do this while suffering through the excruciating pain of an abscessed tooth.

We settled into my office and Brian proceeded to deftly guide me through a maze of story issues. I noticed however that he would pause and hold his cheek for a moment and then say, "It's nothing, let's keep going", and keep going we did. For the next several hours he illustrated story principles, showing me sequences from films like "Tootsie" and "it's a Wonderful Life". I was amazed at his many insights. Gradually my own story was becoming clearer.

At one point, however, his pain had become so great I forced him to let me take him to a dentist. Amazingly during the half hour car ride he continued to share with me more insights on how I might find the key to unlock my story.

Even the next day after x-rays and pain pills we were having lunch discussing story once again with a producer and a story executive. Finally Brian stood up on the verge of fainting from pain, apologizing for not being able to keep going. Mercifully, he found relief from an oral surgeon.

I still marvel when I look at the photos of he and I from that day at the pharmacy and in front of the Disney theatre, smiling... as if he didn't have a care in the world.

Apparently I found that thing that Brian "would rather die than do"... Be forced to give up on helping someone else unlock their own story.

Brian is what you would call "an Old Soul"

with wisdom beyond his years.

Maybe it's because he has spent so much time reflecting on the work of the great film makers

who have laid the foundations we all stand upon today... and yet too often take for granted.

He honors these masters by shining a light on the principles they employed in crafting their classics, men like Frank Capra, Billy Wilder, Alfred Hitchcock and Rod Serling.

He reminds us that they had something to say and if we are to walk in their shoes so should we.

Brian McDonald is an exceedingly rare combination of talent and heart.

He not only is a remarkable teacher, he is also a gifted story teller.

This makes what he has to share that much more valuable. He speaks with passion and experience.

The essays contained in "Ink Spots" are a wonderful breath of fresh air for any film maker, no matter how experienced one may be. I learned my craft of animation from Walt Disney's "Nine Old Men". I know how it feels to have my eyes opened and suddenly "Get it."

I also know that being taught by Brian McDonald feels like that.

—Glen Keane, August 2012

CONTENTS

PART ONE: THINGS I HAVE LEARNED

PART TWO: THOUGHTS ON CRAFT

Introduction

IT IS STRANGE TO BE WRITING an introduction for this book because I started the *Invisible Ink Blog* to help get my first book, *Invisible Ink,* published.

I was having coffee with my friend Michael, and more likely than not I was complaining about either Hollywood or the publishing world. I had written *Invisible Ink* based on classes I'd been teaching for years. I had given out the book to students and had, on my own, received some high-profile endorsements. Still, no one would publish the book.

After a sip of coffee, Michael says to me, "You should have a blog." I didn't want to because it just seemed faddish to me. He said that many people had gotten book deals based on their blogs. I said I would think about it and then promptly forgot all about it.

But a week or two later, I got an email from Michael saying that he had started my blog. All I needed to do was fill it in with content. So I did.

At first, I put up sections of my unpublished book. Then, prompted once again by Michael, I began to write new content just for the blog. Contained within this book are some of those posts.

As I compiled this book, I saw a few patterns emerge. For one, I can't seem to stop talking about August Wilson. He was a remarkable human being and storyteller, and I was lucky to know him. He taught me a lot, so you will notice his name coming up from time to time—not too often, I hope.

You will also notice Rod Serling's name popping up more than once. I never met him—he died when I was ten years old—but no one has taught me more about the responsibility of being a storyteller than Rod. I work hard to fill my work with as much love of humanity as he had in his. When I grow up, I want to be Rod Serling.

Another pattern I have found in my blog postings is the repetition of my dislike of computer-generated special effects. They are part of what has made us lazy storytellers. We lean too heavily on spectacle at the expense of character and plot. In my opinion, our screen stories have become devoid of emotion. Cold. I would welcome these advancements if they were used as tools to help us rather than as crutches to lean on.

There may be more patterns that I have not noticed. If there are, I apologize for the repetition, but I think each post has its own value, as well as a cumulative value.

Ironically, I started the blog to get my first book published, and turns out it is my book that has helped the blog get published as a book. Life is funny.

For those of you who have been followers of the *Invisible Ink Blog*, I thank you. Without you, I would have stopped writing these posts long ago and this book would not exist at all—so you have only yourselves to blame.

If you are a new reader, I hope that you find this content as useful as others have.

Good luck to all of you with your storytelling.

—Brian McDonald, 2011

Part One:
Things I Have Learned

Posted Monday, November 16, 2009

The Rabbit Doesn't Always Win

LAST WEEKEND, I GUEST LECTURED for some friends who co-teach a screenwriting class, and something came up that I see happen a lot. As I taught/spoke, I could see people were working very hard to "get it." They seemed to feel as if they had to understand what I was talking about right then and there.

One of the things that teaching has done for me is to make me a better student, because I see where others get blocked and now know how to look out for these things in myself. Our system of education reinforces the idea that if you get things quickly, you are a better learner than those who don't. This makes us afraid to struggle with a concept. We are afraid of the headache that comes from wrestling with an idea. If it doesn't come quickly, we blame ourselves and sometimes the teacher. But sometimes we just need more time with an idea.

I'm not sure if I should say this, but the truth is that the students who "get it" quickly usually don't "get it" very well at all. Learning this stuff is not a sprint; it's a marathon.

When people think they understand a new concept right away, they stop looking at it, and they never get past the most superficial understanding of it. But anything worth learning is multilayered. Often these are concepts that seem on their surface to be very simple, even simplistic. I promise you that it is these simple ideas that yield the most knowledge. Like a Zen parable, these simple ideas can be pondered for years and can lead to profound discoveries.

But if you think you "got it," then you will never look any deeper. Sometimes, people cut me off when I am talking to let me know that they "got it" and I can move on. Later, these people struggle the most.

I sometimes hand out a list of films for people to watch, and almost always someone tells me that they don't need to see the films on the list because they have seen them before. My class is all about teaching students to look at things differently, to see differently. I often show film clips from movies they are intimately familiar with, and like a magic trick, I reveal to them aspects of the film that they had never noticed before. These aspects are not unimportant minutiae but things of substance that they wonder how they ever missed. I sometimes see people's mouths drop at the revelations. It is these same people, however, who will say that they do not need to see the films on the list.

The people who struggle are trying to see all aspects of the new idea. They are working harder and get more out of it in the end.

I remind students and former students of this all the time—to always be a student. Once you think you "get it," you stop learning. So even when it has been months or years since you've had a big epiphany, if you keep looking, profound things will reveal themselves to you. It may take a while, but as I said, this is a marathon.

If none of this makes sense to you, just think about it for a while—you'll get it.

POSTED TUESDAY, MARCH 28, 2006

ON THE SHOULDERS OF GIANTS

SIR ISAAC NEWTON ONCE SAID, "If I have seen further, it is by standing on the shoulders of giants." He was, of course, referring to the great astronomers who came before him such as Galileo and Kepler. Most physicists believe Newton to be the greatest scientific mind ever in their field, and yet Newton gave the credit for his success to others.

Everyone I know who is good at what they do will speak with great reverence of those who influenced them and their work. August Wilson used to tell me that he wanted to be as good a playwright as Chekhov. Billy Wilder worshiped Ernst Lubitsch and kept a sign above his desk: "What would Lubitsch do?" Paddy Chayefsky said he learned to structure drama by studying Lillian Hellman. Everyone good has their giants, but in the last few years, I have seen that giants are no longer acknowledged. It seems that the younger people are, the more they want to make a mark without doing the work it takes to make that happen. They want to be different—without studying what came before them and without copying the work of the giants who walked the earth before them. That's right, copying. Human beings seem to learn by copying others.

Mike Mignola, the artist who created the popular *Hellboy* comic book series, developed his "unique" drawing style by copying the drawings of artist Frank Frazetta over and over until his own style emerged.

I once heard a radio interview with a musician who had played with the legendary jazz trumpeter Miles Davis. This man had grown up on Davis's music and one day told Miles that when he was a kid, he would play his records over and over again. He said that he would play his trumpet along with the records, trying to sound as much like Miles as possible. Miles laughed and said, "Sometimes it takes a long time to sound like yourself." Nowadays I find that people want to "sound like themselves" without learning to sound like someone else first. They want to skip steps taken by others. Artists want to be Picasso without going through the same steps Picasso took. They want to be innovators, but all innovators stand on the shoulders of giants.

I often tell my students to find what I call a "virtual mentor." That is, they should find two or three giants to copy. *Copy* is not a strong enough word; you should steal from these giants. Picasso said, "Bad artists copy. Great artists steal." When you find these virtual mentors, try to be as much like them as possible, and they will teach you things about your craft that you didn't even know were there to learn. Put a sign above your desk that says, "What would ________ do?" And one day, without even meaning to, you will find that you have learned how to sound like yourself. And you will see just how far you can see when perched atop a giant's shoulders.

POSTED FRIDAY, AUGUST 29, 2008

THE BEST WRITING ADVICE I EVER GOT

ONE THOUSAND YEARS AGO, when I was a teenager, I went to a sci-fi convention in Seattle. This was probably 1978 or 1979. In those days, these kinds of conventions were only attended by hardcore geeks, called nerds in those days, who were on the fringe of society. Big movie stars did not go to these events. The biggest star at this convention was the actor who played Boomer on the original *Battlestar Galactica.*

In attendance were a smattering of comic book creators. And it was while sitting in on a panel with these creators that I heard the best piece of writing advice I have ever heard to this day.

I can't remember who the writer was, though it may have been Steve Englehart, whom I met at that convention and still talk to from time to time.

Whoever it was listened to a story pitch from the crowd and gave back this golden nugget: "If you have a Batman story and you can turn it into a Superman story, it isn't a very good Batman story."

That was it. That was the advice. I use this advice whenever I write.

Some of you will think this is nothing special. Too simplistic. But the mistake of not making a story character-specific is one of the most common mistakes that I see writers make. It may be simple advice, but few people know it or use it.

First you must understand that plot and character are linked. They are one and the same; one does not exist without the other. "Character-driven" is how people describe a story that has no plot but is just an observation of people behaving. There is a reason that this type of story reaches a small audience and is boring to most people. Nothing happens.

On the other end of the spectrum is the story that uses characters who are simply buffeted around by the story. Things happen to them, and character and plot are not really intertwined. These stories may excite people but have little or no emotional impact.

It is the combination of plot and character that makes a story sing. You cannot remove Hamlet from *Hamlet* and replace him with King Lear. Those characters and plots are unified into a single entity.

In *Finding Nemo*, Marlin is an overprotective father who is afraid of the big bad ocean. What happens? His overprotective nature pushes his son to take risks he might not otherwise take, resulting in his being taken away. This means Marlin must face his fear and search the ocean looking for his lost boy.

See how the character is interlocked with the story? They are not separate things.

Characters create plot through their actions or lack thereof. And these actions are driven by the hopes, fears, strengths, weaknesses, desires, loves, hates, or insecurities of these characters. It is how these characters confront or avoid these things that create drama in stories.

In the film *The Wizard of Oz*, Dorothy is not simply a girl who is taken to a faraway land by a twister. No, she is a girl who dreams of life away from her farm. She wants to be somewhere far away. It is this Dorothy who is swept away by the tornado, only to find that she wants nothing more than to go home.

Here again, story and character are linked.

Ask yourself when you write, "Why this character for this story?" Make sure one cannot exist with the other. Can you plug in any generic character to your story? Character and plot are respectively the body and soul of stories—the yin and yang. Make sure you don't have a Batman story that can just as easily be a Superman story.

If you follow this piece of advice, the quality of your work will be consistent and will appeal to more people.

POSTED SATURDAY, OCTOBER 31, 2009

HERE THERE BE MONSTERS

ONE OF THE MOST COMMON CONCERNS I hear from people about the application of story structure to their work is that they fear their writing will become stiff and mechanical. They are right. I will not argue with them about that.

This argument, however, is made primarily by those who have a hard time understanding and applying story structure, and it is convenient for them to say that it makes their work mechanical.

This is true of the process of learning anything. Most people who learn to play the piano start with the simple tune "Chopsticks" and move on to something like "Twinkle, Twinkle, Little Star." When they are first learning these songs, they do not produce anything that sounds very much like music. It's more like a series of unrelated notes. But sure enough, after much practice, the notes begin to sound more and more like an actual song. And some of these people go on to play or create great music.

Why would this be any different from learning to structure a story? It isn't. When one is learning story structure, one's writing goes from clumsy and clunky to seemingly effortless. There is still effort, but those early lessons have moved into the subconscious. You learn these things so deeply after years of practice that you take for granted that you know them.

I remember trying to learn the guitar years ago. I remember how hard it was to make my fingers do the right things. I had to think so hard about where to place my fingers. It was not fun, and it did not sound like music. But people who stick with it learn so well where their fingers go that it recedes to the back of their minds.

This is where you want to get with writing and constructing stories. You have to be prepared to be bad. I tell my students that they have to love this enough to be bad at it.

That is why I can't play a musical instrument. I did not love it enough to be bad at it. I didn't like that the guitar made my fingers hurt or that what I was playing sounded like mistakes. I wanted to make music, but I wasn't willing to do the work that it takes to make music.

I'm reminded of an early art teacher for the late, great animation director Chuck Jones, who was fond of telling his students that they all had 100,000 bad drawings inside them, and the sooner they got them out, the better.

If you have acquired any kind of mastery of some skill, chances are you did not start off great. You may have, if you were lucky, had a natural talent for it. But talent takes you only so far, and soon enough, you hit the edge of your natural abilities. I have seen many, many people stop at that edge, afraid to go over. This is like an old-fashioned sailor's map that said of unknown areas, "Here there be monsters." It's the edge of the world.

But if you sail beyond that edge, there is a new world. This is where you learn to appreciate the challenges that come with an opportunity to learn and grow.

Don't be afraid to be bad at this for a while. Don't be afraid to sail off the earth you know. There are no monsters here.

Posted Monday, April 27, 2009

My Bad Play and What It Taught Me

"Never bore people."
—*Billy Wilder*

WHEN I WAS IN THE EIGHTH GRADE, I was a big *Star Trek* fan. At that time, there was no movie and no Next Generation, just the original *Trek* in reruns and the cartoon series that got me hooked in the first place. Anyway, the show was—and continues to be—a big influence on my writing.

Back then, I was in a drama class, and we had to write a short play and perform it for our parents.

I decided to write a *Star Trek* episode. I had so much fun writing the episode. Here I was, able to put words in the mouths of characters I loved so much. The script just spilled out of me, it was so easy to write. It was fun—really fun—to do.

I turned in my script, and parts were assigned to my fellow thespians. I, of course, played the captain, which was also fun.

We rehearsed it. It was even more fun to see the thing come to life.

The big night came when it was time to put on the show for our parents. We had our lines memorized and our cool retro-1960s costumes on as we waited in the wings to go out there and share all this fun with the people in the audience.

It was time. The curtain rose, and we started to put on what I thought was the best episode of *Star Trek* ever.

We were putting our all into it. And yes, we were having lots of fun. How could you not have fun playing Kirk, being out there on the stage "Kirking" it up?

Then it happened. I looked out in the crowd and saw someone's dad nodding off. He was trying to stay awake, but it was a Herculean task for the poor man. His head would fall slowly until his chin was on his chest, and then he would jerk it up again with his eyes wide open. But in a few moments, his head would fall again.

All I could think was, *How can he be bored?* The show had been so much fun to write and perform, how could it not be just as much fun to watch?

I learned a very important lesson that night. Just because it was fun for you to create doesn't mean it will be fun for your audience to watch.

I was lucky to learn this lesson young. Some people never learn it. They get so caught up in their creative world that the audience is an afterthought. They may also have a tendency to blame the audience in a very sour grapes kind of way. They say things like, "They're not smart enough to get it," or "I'm ahead of my time."

This thinking does nothing to help you master your craft. It is not selling out to attempt to communicate with your audience. It has become an artistic crime to strive to communicate clearly with all of one's audience. People will say that it is pandering. They will say that it is appealing to the lowest common denominator. They tend to think that a boring, confusing movie is better than one that moves or emotionally engages the audience. For them, it is the highest form of art to have people scratching their heads when they walk away.

I have never understood why people think it takes great craftsmanship to confuse and/or bore the audience. If this is the case, I mastered scriptwriting my first time out. If that dad in the audience is any indication, I was an eighth-grade genius.

The truth is that it is very hard to make yourself understood. I was at a book reading at a bookstore a while ago, and someone asked the author why she didn't write more books. She said, "It takes a long time to write something that is easy to read."

Every time I sit down to write something, I think of that dad jerking his head up as he fought off sleep. It keeps me honest. It keeps me from being self-indulgent. It keeps the audience in my head. I try to view the piece through their eyes instead of just my own.

I'm not saying I never bored anybody; I'm just saying I try hard not to.

All writers should be so lucky as to stand before an audience and bore them to sleep with their precious words. It was painful and embarrassing, but I sure am glad it happened.

POSTED MONDAY, AUGUST 23, 2010

WORKING HARD FOR THE MONEY

MY STEPFATHER ONCE TOLD ME when I was a kid that what made someone a professional rather than an amateur was that they were paid for what they did. He was wrong.

Many people use my stepfather's explanation for what makes a professional, and I find that it leads to shoddy workmanship because it takes the focus off getting good at what we do and shifts it to getting good enough to get paid—or even worse, *just* getting paid. Craft is often thrown out the window in favor of just doing whatever it takes to get paid.

I meet people all the time who are very interested in becoming screenwriters or filmmakers, but they have almost no interest in the craft itself. They want money or fame or some other outward indication of success, but the idea that they should be able to do good work, and do it consistently, is beyond them.

This is not to say they don't want to do good work. The problem is that they assume their work is good simply by virtue of having been made by them. The work needs to meet no other standard.

When I talk to these people about standards of quality or craft that takes years to master, they shrug it off. That takes too long. Learning. Mastering. They just want the money, and I make it sound like too much work.

My friend Pat Hazell talks about talking to writers starting out who are obsessed with getting an agent. His response is always,

"What do you have for them to sell?" It's amazing how often they have nothing.

August Wilson once told me that people used to ask him how they could get a play on Broadway. He would then ask them if they had a play, and they would often say no. He would tell them to write a play and then write another play. He told them to keep writing plays. He told me that they would get mad at him, as if he had a secret he wasn't telling them. The truth is that the secret is always hard work. And if they had something they knew needed work, he always told them that their plays had to be as good as they could make them.

If you think your script (or whatever product) could be better, then why do you think you should be able to sell it?

You have to learn to feel rewarded by the quality of your own work and not to be delusional about it.

One trick is to study the classics and compare your work to those. Most people see a bad film and say, "I could write that." But if you are only trying to be as good as the worst thing you have ever seen, you aren't doing yourself any favors.

Compare your work to the best work you can find. Write as closely as you can to that level.

Another great trick is to get your script as good as you can get it, then print it out, bind it, and hand it to someone you trust to read it. A strange thing will happen. As soon as you hand it to someone to read, you become aware of everything that is wrong with the script. Those things that were nagging you—that you thought you could get away with—will become very clear to you. Fix those things. Even before you get notes from a reader, fix those things.

Work, work, work on this stuff until it's as good as you can get it. If you want to sell a screenplay for one million dollars, put in a million dollars' worth of work.

To put it simply, one is not a professional when one gets paid. One becomes a professional and *then* gets paid.

Posted Tuesday, March 13, 2007

Get Rich Quick! Become a Hollywood Screenwriter!

"Opportunity is missed by most people because it is dressed in overalls and looks like work."
—*Thomas Edison*

I WAS ONCE ASKED TO SHOW a short film of mine and speak about filmmaking at a community college. At the time, my film—a short film called *White Face*—had been running on HBO. After a few standard questions such as "What was the budget?" and "How long did it take to make?" came a question that floored me. A young man raised his hand and asked, "How do I get my film on HBO?" For me, the assumption behind that question verged on an insult.

Why? Because it devalued my craft. Filmmaking has become the get-rich-quick scheme of our times. The problem with get-rich-quick schemes is that they promise great success with minimum effort. One of the things I dig about my friends who draw is that they are aware that it takes time and effort to get good.

Once at a Comic-Con in San Diego, a bunch of artists I knew were looking at someone's portfolio, their mouths agape. They oohed and aahed for a while, then someone asked how old the artist was. The answer came back that he was forty-five or so, and with that, they all relaxed and nodded. They were relieved because they understood he had put his time in.

Imagine a person who has never picked up a paintbrush deciding that they want to be an artist. Upon completing their first painting, they call the Louvre and other museums and ask the curators if they would be interested in purchasing and displaying their masterpiece. Sounds silly, right? Yet people have no problem believing that they should sell their first screenplay or have their first film distributed.

I have the utmost respect for the people I know who draw because they understand that talent is nothing if not backed up by skill, and skill takes time and effort to acquire. What bothers me about some younger people wanting to break into films is their sense of entitlement. They don't seem to care about the craft of filmmaking, only the fame and/or money. They know nothing about the history of the craft they wish to enter and have never seen the films of John Ford, John Huston, Frank Capra, David Lean, Howard Hawks, or Billy Wilder. These legends have things to teach, but few bother to listen. They just want to know who they can call and what the next step is to becoming famous.

I once had an aspiring filmmaker tell me she was on a quest to find out how to involve an audience. She said there must be some key to keeping an audience interested in your film. I told her to read Hitchcock interviews because he was probably the most articulate filmmaker in history when it comes to engaging audiences. She scoffed at that, saying she didn't like Hitchcock and didn't think he would have anything to teach her.

I know quite a few people who have done well in the movie business, but they all had a minimum of ten years of hard work under their belts before anyone bothered to pay attention to them. These people were not no-talent hacks. They had talent, and after years of hard work, they are now show biz VIPs. I knew them when no one of consequence would return their calls, come see them perform, or read their screenplays. But they just kept doing what they were doing, and they acquired skills.

Jerry Seinfeld tells a story about how he was looking out a window one morning and saw construction workers on their way to work. He thought to himself, "If those guys can get up in the morning and go to work, I should be able to do the same with my work." So he began getting up early in the morning and sitting down for a couple of hours each day to write jokes. Johnny Carson was so used to getting up, reading the paper, and writing jokes that he even did it after he retired.

If you are unwilling to see filmmaking or screenwriting as a craft you must hone, you will fall behind your competitors who are willing to work a little harder. If you are unwilling to study the work of those who came before you, you will fall behind your competitors who are willing to learn. Most of all, if you think this business is a way to get rich quick, you are in for a world of heartbreak.

I once heard Steve Martin give a young comic this advice: "Be so good they can't ignore you." Good advice, but it takes work to be that good. If you are unwilling to do that work, find a craft that you are willing to work at and do that.

All I have ever wanted in my life is to be good at what I do and be paid for it. While I was making my film *White Face,* HBO could not have been further from my mind. I was only trying to make a good film. Having the film run on HBO did not bring me fame or fortune; it was just one brick on the road to wherever I end up in this business. Meanwhile, I am working on getting better.

So my advice to the young man who wants a film on HBO? Make a film good enough to be on HBO, and they will call you. Even if they don't, you will have something you can be proud of. And for that, you can be proud of yourself.

Posted Monday, November 13, 2006

The Artist's Vision

"But why do you want to build an amusement park? They're so dirty."

—*Walt Disney's wife, on his idea for Disneyland*

FOR THOSE OF US BORN AFTER 1955, it is difficult to imagine a world without Disneyland. But for the people who were born on the other side of that year, it was just as difficult to imagine a world with Disneyland in it. Mrs. Disney was correct; amusement parks were dirty places. She could not conceive of them being otherwise, and neither could anyone else. Except Walt.

In the late 1920s, Walt Disney had made his name making funny little cartoons about a mouse. It is almost impossible for us to understand the enormous popularity of Mickey Mouse in those days. Mickey Mouse was a bona fide movie star. Before the first Mickey Mouse cartoon hit the movie screens, Walt was told that it was a bad idea to try to "popularize a mouse."

A few years later, Walt had an idea to make a feature-length cartoon. Everyone thought it was a terrible idea. No one could imagine an audience sitting through a cartoon that long. In Hollywood, his project was called "Disney's Folly." He was expected to lose his shirt. The film turned out to be *Snow White and the Seven Dwarfs,* and it was a smash. Just as with Disneyland, it became impossible to imagine a world without Disney's version of *Snow White*. Going further, can one imagine a world without feature-length animated films?

One of the things that make a person an artist is their ability to look at the world and see what is missing. They can visualize in their mind's eye a brand new thing or see an old thing in a completely different way from others around them. They have vision. But more often than not, people do not trust a visionary artist.

When Francis Ford Coppola was hired to adapt the novel *The Godfather,* the studio worried that they had made a mistake. In his head, Coppola had a vision for the film that did not match anyone else's. Every decision he made was questioned. The studio did not want Marlon Brando in the cast. Nor did they want Al Pacino in the part of Michael; they suggested Robert Redford. The director of photography, Gordon Willis, is now known as one of the best in the world, but at the time, the studio thought his photography was too dark. The studio even went so far as to hire another director to follow Coppola around so that when they fired him, this new director could step right in.

Coppola's *The Godfather* is now regarded as one of the best films of all time.

George Lucas's film *American Graffiti* became a cultural phenomenon despite the fact that the studio expected it to lose money. They could not see what Lucas saw. Following the success of *American Graffiti,* Lucas went to all of the studios with a new project called *Star Wars.* No one expected much of the film, and everyone but 20th Century Fox turned it down. Even Fox didn't think enough of the film to retain merchandising and sequel rights. Lucas kept those. After an early private screening of the film, all of George's friends told him he had failed. Lucas's wife Marcia purportedly cried because she thought George had wasted too much time on this piece of garbage.

In May 1977, *Star Wars* became the most popular film in the galaxy.

In the late 1950s, Alfred Hitchcock started work on a film about a transvestite murderer called *Psycho.* Longtime associates distanced themselves from the film and decided not to work with Hitchcock on this one. "You've gone too far, Hitch," they said. Universal Studios also felt he had gone too far and gave the legendary director a minuscule budget. Hitchcock put up his own house as collateral to get the money to make the film. *Psycho* is now a classic.

I wrote these stories down so you artists out there will stick to your creative guns. I want you to realize that if you have a clear vision of something truly new, it may not be recognized by the people in power or those around you. The world is full of naysayers who cannot see what you see until after it's done. Sometimes the entire world is against you, but neither their power nor their numbers make them right.

"When a true genius appears, you may know him by this sign: that all the dunces are in a confederacy against him."
—Jonathan Swift

Posted Sunday, August 5, 2007

The Secret of Magic

YEARS AGO, A GOOD FRIEND OF MINE was an apprentice film editor at the same time that he was learning carpentry from his father. One day, the film editor says to my friend, "When you read about carpentry, think about editing."

My friend and I talked about this for some time, trying to figure out what the film editor meant. We were both in our late teens at the time and couldn't make sense of it. Now that I'm older, I see what he meant was that the principles of one craft can be applied to another.

Even people who have mastered their craft can gain valuable insights by looking closely at someone else's.

On BBC America, I watch master chef Gordon Ramsay on his show *Kitchen Nightmares*. He takes failing restaurants and helps the owners revamp their businesses. More often than not, he finds two related problems: 1) the chefs at these places let ego get in the way of their work, and 2) they make the dishes too complex.

Ramsay's struggle is to get these chefs to simplify their dishes. This is exactly the same thing I find with less experienced screenwriters, filmmakers, and comic book illustrators. They tend to be much more into style than the foundations of their respective crafts. Youth often goes for style over substance. As a teacher, it helps me to see Chef Ramsay deal with the same problems I deal with but in an entirely different universe.

Speaking of an entirely different universe, learning magic has been unbelievably helpful in helping me gain a deeper understanding of my craft. In my teaching, I have found that students often dismiss something because it is too simple. They often think what you teach them will never work because an audience will surely see through something so elementary. In learning magic, I have seen myself have the same reaction as my students. Most magic tricks are quite simple—at least in principle. They might be hard to master, but the methods behind them are so simple that when you read the description, you think there is no way a person could be fooled—but they are. In fact, the simpler the trick, the more fantastic the illusion.

I am an amateur magician. A few months ago, I did a trick for some friends and screwed it up. They were not impressed. This was a trick I had done before that had blown people away. But because I screwed it up, my friends could not believe that it could have ever worked. They were polite. They said that it might be a good trick... for kids.

When I teach students to set things up in the first act that will pay off later, they complain that it is too predictable to do things that way. Like the simple magic trick, they think that it will never work. They have all seen too many bad films where they could see how everything returns and works out. But this is like my poorly executed trick: only poor craftsmanship is at fault, not the method itself.

Among other things, learning the craft of magic has taught me to trust the methods and to know that it is up to me to perform them well. My advice to you is to master a simple magic trick or two just to see how something so simple can amaze an audience. And when you read about magic, think about screenwriting. You'll be surprised at what you discover.

Posted Thursday, October 23, 2008

The Perfect Solution

I WOULD LIKE TO TAKE BACK the word *perfectionist*. Let's start by assuming that perfection is something we can actually attain. For instance, some people say that there is no such thing as a perfect circle. But for all practical purposes, there is. Let's say near perfect is perfect.

Why am I defining perfection? Because I have seen many screenwriters and others use unattainable perfection as a false goal that allows them to procrastinate. How many of you have been working on "that project" for years? Chances are you are afraid to move forward because when the project is done, it will not be "perfect."

Ultimately, you're afraid of judgment—your own or someone else's. Someone may see your mistakes, and you will be confronted with your shortcomings. As long as the project exists only in your head, it is an uncompromised ideal.

Perfection is a way not to finish. It is a way not to make decisions because you might make the wrong decision. It is a way not to be judged. But being judged is a part of being an artist. If you are unwilling to take this risk, you cannot be an artist.

If you do the best job you possibly can, then by definition, you can do no better. This is when you stop, because this is as close as any of us can get to perfection.

This quest for the unattainable creates the illusion of progression without the results. In his novel *The Plague,* Albert Camus created a would-be novelist, Joseph Grand, who ceaselessly revised his first sentence, never getting beyond it.

The thing to remember is that all artists share this fear that they will produce crap that everyone hates. Usually, only the worst artists do not have this fear.

Years ago, I was at Comic-Con in San Diego with my friend Brian O'Connell. Brian is an illustrator and director over at Lucasfilm working on the *Star Wars: The Clone Wars* television show. But at the time, he was just a guy trying to break into comics who was being passed over by know-nothing comic book editors who could not see his talent.

One of the people who could see his talent was a very famous comic book artist I will not name here. This artist saw Brian's work and was so impressed that he showed us some pages for his new comic book, which no one had heard of yet but would soon become a phenomenon. But at this point, he had not even finished the first book. Brian and I were blown away. These were truly beautiful pages.

Brian thought he'd make a joke and said with a straight face, "You need to work on your proportions."

The famous artist got a sheepish look on his face and said, "Yeah, I know." Brian had to explain that he was just joking and that the pages were amazing.

Even this very successful artist, who is very, very good, has his doubts about his work. But this doubt does not stop him from creating. Don't let it stop you. Understand that the imperfect work you produce is far better than the perfect work that lives only in your head. Sit down and get it done.

If you work hard, the next thing will be better, and the next thing will be better still—which is perfect.

Posted Friday, September 24, 2010

You Don't Know What You Don't Know

"Everybody is ignorant, only on different subjects."
—*Will Rogers*

IN MY LIFE, I HAVE KNOWN MANY ARTISTS who dismiss the idea of structure when it comes to art. It doesn't feel organic for them to work with a plan or to impose a form on their art. They believe that their art will lose emotional power. This is a mistake.

I was once invited to see the one-woman show of an actress I know. She's a really good actress: smart, funny, quick, talented, and skilled. She gave me tickets to her show and said that following the show, there would be a Q&A. I went to the show along with two guests.

Before the show began, the theater was packed and abuzz with anticipation. This actress has quite a local following, and people expected to be thoroughly entertained.

They were not disappointed. The show was funny and engaging, and after a spectacular crescendo, the lights came up to thunderous applause.

People took this time to grab some fresh air and, for some, to smoke in front of the theater.

My friends and I talked about how much we liked the show and debated whether to stay for the Q&A. I thought that I should because the actress did give me free tickets. We stayed, but many people did not. More than half of the audience left.

We sat back down expecting the Q&A, but the lights dimmed and, much to our surprise, there was a second part to the show.

When that ended, the Q&A followed. During the Q&A, my friend the actress commented on the audience that had left at intermission. She said something to the effect of, "Some people get what I do, and some people just don't get it."

This is not an unusual reaction for an artist who works strictly from the gut—it is the "they don't get me" defense. There are times when that can be true, but mostly it's the artist who doesn't "get it," not the audience.

Thousands of years of conditioning have taught us the natural shape of a story.

If you don't understand that this is so, you may not be clear on just what you are communicating to your audience.

People will often tell me that a film is well structured but that it is too long. I don't believe that there is any such thing as too long. Some of the longest films I have ever seen are short films.

But when a story is aimless and meandering, people have no idea of its shape, and they become uneasy. How many times have you felt as if a film was going to end, only to have it continue for another twenty, thirty, or sixty minutes? Each minute past the time when you thought the film was over is a minute too long. It's poor structure.

If you understand structure, you can use people's expectations to your advantage. I'm not talking about breaking rules so much as bending them.

If you look at James Cameron's film *Aliens*, he makes use of audience expectations to create a false ending. There is a fiery climax followed by what appears to be a wrap-up. But we soon find out that this story is not quite finished.

Why did this work when my friend's false climax did not? It's because the story did not truly resolve. At the beginning of *Aliens,* Ripley is haunted by nightmares of aliens. Ripley must do battle with the monster of the story. She must conquer her fear by confronting it in the form of this alien. After this final battle, she is finally free of these dreams. The end.

What my actress friend failed to realize is that she communicated to us that her show was over. Her show came to a conclusion of an idea, culminating with a climax. She told us it was over. But because she did not understand what she had done, she could only blame the viewers.

Understanding the basics of story structure would have helped her to keep her audience, and it will help you to keep yours.

POSTED SUNDAY, OCTOBER 12, 2008

OUR VERY OWN LIBRARY OF ALEXANDRIA

THE LIBRARY OF ALEXANDRIA was the largest library in the ancient world. The aim of this ancient Egyptian library was to collect the world's knowledge. It was said that when foreign ships came into port, their books and all written materials were confiscated, copied, and returned to their owners.

The library was tragically destroyed in a fire. Scholars still lament the loss of this vast repository of knowledge. What would we know if we had this ancient information at our fingertips?

I am old enough to remember the advent of the VCR. The idea that you could tape a show and watch it later or keep it forever was amazing. But even more amazing was the idea that you could watch whatever movie you wanted, when you wanted. For a boy like me, who since the age of five had wanted to be a filmmaker, this was not a mere piece of technology but a gift from the gods.

When Orson Welles wanted to learn how to make films, he screened John Ford's film *Stagecoach* over and over again. Before the VCR, this required a film print and projector. For most people, this was cost-prohibitive. Other students of film would have to sit through multiple screenings of a movie in order to study it. And in those days, when a film left the theater, that was it. There was no cable. There was no VCR, DVD, or Blu-ray. When a film was gone, it was gone. If you were lucky, you might see it on TV. But even then, it would be cut up to make it family-friendly and to allow for commercials.

But with the VCR, any young student of film could do just what Orson Welles had done. I dreamed about how the VCR would advance the craft of filmmaking because now we all had the history of film at our disposal.

Think of it: the history of film is just over a hundred years old, and much of the best work by the best filmmakers in history is available to us. This is our Library of Alexandria.

Our teachers can be Eisenstein, Griffith, Chaplin, Keaton, Capra, Ford, Kurosawa, Hawks, Welles, Lean, Wilder, Hitchcock, Wellman, Wyler, Huston, Stevens, Lumet, Ritt, Cukor, Kazan, Bergman, Pollack, Peckinpah, Donen, Logan, Rydell, LeRoy, Forman, Preminger, Penn, Milestone, Minnelli, Kramer, Wise, Lang, Ashby, Zinnemann, Hiller, Vidor, Lubitsch, and countless more.

Yet I am constantly amazed when talking to younger film students that they have seen almost no classic cinema. They are put off by black-and-white photography or some other superficial aspect of old films. Why let something so small stop you from learning from the best? People who study physics still study Newton and Einstein. They understand and respect that those who came before have something to teach them.

The Library of Alexandria still has something to teach us. We cannot take for granted the vast store of knowledge we have at our disposal. As filmmakers, why not take the opportunity to learn from those who came before us? It is the best way to go further than they did.

PART TWO:
THOUGHTS ON CRAFT

Posted Friday, February 19, 2010

How to Be Original

ONE OF THE PROBLEMS I RUN INTO a lot when teaching story structure is the question of originality. People want to know how they will ever be original if they follow the time-honored principles of structure.

When people say these things, I know they are far more interested in the glory and praise of creativity than the roll-up-your-sleeves work of it. They are imagining themselves on the red carpet before the fawning fans and critics. And all before bothering to learn their craft. The aspiration to be good takes a backseat to being praised as a genius and living a Warhol-like existence. And this is of course your reward for doing something new and different. Or so many think.

I have written stories that people told me were "original." I can assure you that that was not my goal at all. I just wanted to do good work, following the lead of those who came before me. If Chaplin or Hitchcock or Wilder—or Jim Henson or Bruce Lee or Chuck Jones or John Ford or any number of masters—says to do it, then that's what I will do.

My goal is always to be as good as I can be. I want to communicate clearly with my audience, engage them, and touch them in some way. I have no problem using tools that have worked since time immemorial. In all of my reading, I have found that the masters were all trying to do the same thing—to do the best they could. Being good is hard enough without trying to be unprecedented.

You've probably heard lots of talk about how much *Avatar* is like *Dances with Wolves*. Yes, it has similarities. But there is not one story anywhere that cannot be traced, in part, to an earlier source.

The infant Moses was set adrift so that his life would be spared, and he was adopted and raised by strangers and became a hero. Same as Superman.

Zorro and Batman are the same; both are rich men who fight crime in costumes. No matter what you try to do, someone has already done a version of it. Trust me.

There really is nothing new under the sun. Things may look different to the untrained eye, but humanity only has so many emotions and so many concerns. We need food, shelter, and love. We all must live under some form of government. We must all fight our internal demons.

There are no new problems, only the same old problems dressed differently. Take the story of John Henry. Here is an American myth about a man who races against a steam-powered hammer to dig a tunnel through a mountain.

This story comes from the fear people had in the late 1800s that they would be replaced by machines. We have had a strange relationship with machines ever since we started to use them. We build them to make our lives easier, but then we worry that they will replace us. *The Terminator* taps into the very same fear. It's just dressed up in new clothes.

Here's the key to being original: be good and be true to yourself. Originality is often tied to the idea of style. Will Eisner, legendary comic book writer and artist, said that style is what happens as a result of how one solves problems. Style is not something you have to force or invent. Style comes out of you because you yourself are unique.

It's amazing what happens when you rid yourself of the burden of being original. You can breathe easier and get down to the business of doing good work.

If you do this and you do work that matters to you—and if you say the things that matter to you—sometimes you will hit on a new way to combine old ideas, but only in a way that serves your point and only as a result of how you solve problems. Originality is not the goal; it is the product of doing great work.

There is only one you. Originality rises from that. Now that you understand, worry about being good, and let originality take care of itself.

Posted Wednesday, January 28, 2009
Two Questions That Drive Me Crazy

FIRST, SOME BACKSTORY. When I was a kid, there were no VCRs. Only rich people had them; they were still rare for the rest of us. I desperately wanted to see my favorite television shows over and over again, but there was no way to do it, so I used a cassette recorder to record the shows' audio. I would listen to them in bed when I was supposed to be asleep. This was when I was aged ten, eleven, and twelve.

I was a kid obsessed with movies and television and how stories were put together. I needed to know what made a story work. After listening to my recordings of *The Mary Tyler Moore Show, The Bob Newhart Show,* reruns of *The Twilight Zone,* and others, I began to see patterns. I didn't yet know the terms for three-act structure and had never heard of Aristotle, but I knew that the first part of a story was a setup for what was going to come later and that there needed to be some kind of conclusion where it all paid off.

When I was a little older, I found out where I could get screenplays. I got them and read them until I could see the patterns there as well. By the time I started to read books on screenwriting, they were just confirming and putting labels on things I had already observed on my own.

Later, when there were VCRs, I watched movies and studied them over and over again so I could understand the visual language of film. I checked out a 16 mm projector from the public library along with old silent movies and projected them from my room onto the side of a white house next door.

I made my first film at age ten when I met a kid who had a Super 8 camera. All I remember thinking at the time was, "Finally, I'm getting to make a film!" This was something I had wanted to do since I was five and found out you could do such a thing.

When I was thirteen, I saw that there was a listing for motion pictures in my local phone book, so I started calling people and asking questions. That got me my first after-school job as an assistant animation camera operator for a man named Bruce Walters, who taught me things I still use to this day.

Why this trip down memory lane? Because I have two pet peeves.

Beginners often ask me which screenwriting software I use. All I can think is that this is the last thing they need to worry about. They never ask if they have the skill or talent to write a screenplay. Writing screenplays is a lot of work, and the more you understand how to do it, the harder it gets.

But software is always the first question people ask about nowadays. They will not put in the time and effort to hone their craft, but they will plop down a couple hundred bucks on a program that makes their jumble of ideas look like a screenplay.

Sure, every now and then an ex-stripper decides to write a movie and hits the big time. But more often than not, I'm guessing that someone starts off wanting to be a screenwriter and ends up a stripper, not the other way around. This is a tough business, and it helps to study the craft.

The other question has to do with passion.

I often find myself speaking or teaching a class where I tell people that if they want to write screenplays, they should read screenplays. I am surprised at how few people bother to read things written in the form they profess to want to work in. So I say, "Read screenplays." The response that always comes back: "Where do you get screenplays?"

I got my hands on screenplays in the early 1980s when they were much harder but not impossible to find. Back then, not everyone wanted to write movies, so not many people sold screenplays. Now you can get them everywhere.

"Where do we get screenplays?" may sound like an innocent question, but what it really says is that the person is unwilling to put any effort into learning their craft—not even the effort it takes to type "screenplay" into a search engine. C'mon, people.

I once asked a group if they would like to sell a script for a million dollars. They did. "Well," I told them, "if you want to sell something for a million dollars, you have to do a million dollars' worth of work."

No program will help you write better, and a "good idea" is not just proper formatting away from being a hit screenplay. If you want to write screenplays, you have to read screenplays. If you feel you have nothing to learn, then you have no idea how much you really don't know. If you feel you just have a few things to learn, you also have no idea how much you need to learn.

When you sit down to write a screenplay and are gripped with fear and insecurity, when you feel you know nothing, when you know what you don't know, and when you can see there is a mountain you must climb ahead of you, then you are on your way to becoming a screenwriter.

There is only one way to scale this mountain: study your craft. Be a ravenous consumer of information. You can start right now by typing "screenplays" into Google.

POSTED WEDNESDAY, SEPTEMBER 5, 2007

THE ULTIMATE SOPHISTICATION

"Simplicity is the ultimate sophistication."
—*Leonardo da Vinci*

DA VINCI'S QUOTE ON THE SOPHISTICATION of simplicity has been all but forgotten by creative people today. Screenwriting students more than anything else don't want their work to appear too simplistic, too "obvious." The idea of communicating clearly with one's audience is now equated with talking down to them.

Good art, we think, must challenge the viewer to get its meaning. If we can understand something at first glance, we feel it must be without enduring merit, that it is not profound. Note that the responsibility for communication has moved from the creator to the audience. The artist is now free to do whatever comes to mind without the hindrance of clarity. Viewers can be blamed for any breakdown in communication. They were not up to the complexity of the art.

Being clear is an artistic crime nowadays. Steven Spielberg is public enemy number one according to some critics. Spielberg "hits you over the head," they say. If everyone understands his work, how good could it possibly be? I am at a loss as to where the craftsmanship is in deliberately making something convoluted and difficult to comprehend. A five-year-old's story or painting can be personally expressive (and hard to make sense of). But few children, however creative, can reproduce an intended effect with any precision. It takes years of practice to acquire the marksmanship required to hit one's target squarely on the nose.

It is ironic that when a complicated subject is expressed so well that it is understood easily, it is assumed the ease came with the idea. People confuse the ease with which the idea is received with the idea itself being pedestrian. Students of screenwriting or filmmaking rarely marvel at the clarity with which something has been communicated, and film schools seem to help foster the idea that clear communication is unsophisticated. They mainly study "art films" that are slow and hard to follow, with a convoluted story that bravely tackles an important topic.

Lately, I find audiences don't expect to understand what they see. I overheard someone say that they liked the film *Transformers,* with the caveat that it was a typical action movie where you couldn't follow the story. When did incomprehensible plots become typical in action movies? Did the first *Die Hard* (1988) confuse anyone? Take "important" films like *Syriana* or *Babel.* Over and over again, people who saw them told me that the movie was confusing and hard to follow—but good. I can't help but think that "good" here is synonymous with the "good effort!" note that kids get on their school papers.

The primary job of a storyteller is to tell the story clearly. Clarity is where truth comes from. Without that, a story is "just" a story, quickly forgotten. If the filmmaker is absolved of any responsibility to be clear and the viewer must bear the burden of creating meaningful connections, the story is no longer about an audience sharing a truth. It is about individuals in that audience—who really "gets it" and who doesn't.

The most complex story can be broken down into simple elements. That is the work; that is what we all sweat over. The reward is an understanding that seems to come easily. All I ask is that next time a story you can't follow makes you wonder if your brain has turned to mush, turn it around and give yourself some credit for being intelligent. Maybe it isn't your fault. Maybe the storyteller just wasn't sophisticated enough to rely on the strength of simplicity.

Posted Thursday, December 20, 2007

Turn Up the Contrast

I OFTEN HEAR PEOPLE SAY how much they love a film because it is "dark." They wax poetic about dark films because they feel that they are more true-to-life than one that is lighter (or "sappy," as they might say). I feel as if I have asked them what they see in an inkblot. Over many years, I have noticed that these people tend to be gloomier all around. They believe anything good or happy is false, a lie. This is the filter through which they view both life and art.

On the other hand, there are those people who don't want to see any of the dark side of life in their films. They ignore these things in life as well. This group might see two people kissing in their inkblot while the first set sees one person strangling another.

As is often the case, the truth is somewhere in between—light and dark, good and bad are polarities that don't exist without each other. One is no more real or truthful than the other.

Frank Capra, one of my favorite filmmakers, was often accused of being too sweet and sappy. When he was making films, some critics dubbed them "Capra corn." That put-down has stuck. What people seem to forget is that his films get as dark as much as cheery. In *It's a Wonderful Life,* we learn George Bailey is about to kill himself. This is a "feel-good" film, and yet the good-guy main character has a suicidal breakdown.

Watch the film again and see how dark it gets. Sure, it ends on a high note, but if you remember, George Bailey has always wanted to travel the world. When the film ends, he still hasn't gotten to travel.

He probably won't ever travel. He never gets what he wants; he simply learns to appreciate what he has.

In an argument about *Schindler's List*, a friend of mine voiced the opinion of many people (and maybe even a few of you) when he said, "Leave it to Spielberg to make a feel-good movie about the Holocaust." Yes, there were moments in the film that were lighter in tone, but there were also moments in that movie that are about as dark as things can get: children hiding out in a latrine to save their lives, and the entire Kristallnacht sequence where the Nazis cleared the Jewish ghetto.

If these things make you "feel good," seek therapy. You would be hard pressed to find anything as dark in a popular American film.

It seems, as with *It's a Wonderful Life*, that if the story ends on a high point, it is perceived as all light no matter what has happened prior. And the same is true in reverse; a down ending leaves people feeling as though the entire story was dark when it may in fact have had several lighter moments.

But light and dark define one another; one cannot see one without the other. Having an all-dark story is like typing black letters on black paper: it obscures your point. In her insightful book *Picture This: How Pictures Work*, author Molly Bang puts it like this: "Contrast allows us to see." This is a design principle that works for designing stories as well as anything else. Contrast is the best way to make your point clear.

In another Christmas classic, *A Christmas Carol*, Ebenezer Scrooge is seen in his office. It is a cold place, both literally and emotionally. Scrooge would rather let his employee, Bob Cratchit, freeze than put another lump of coal on the fire. The story later shows Scrooge earlier in life when he worked for someone else, a man named Mr. Fezziwig. Fezziwig's place was full of life, warmth, and joy—the exact opposite of Scrooge's. Seeing these two environments in contrast allows each to be seen more clearly.

This idea of contrast is why drama works well in the world of extremes. In a well-told story, a very rich man becomes very poor or vice versa. But if a rich man loses just a little money, it is of little interest to an audience. It illuminates nothing. If a poor man finds a nickel, it is not as interesting as if he wins the lottery. We have a term for this kind of contrast: rags to riches.

Aristotle referred to this as a reversal of the dramatic situation (*peripeteia*). He said that simple plots tend to have no such reversals, whereas complex plots do. A change of fortune for the hero engages and entertains an audience, Aristotle pointed out. What he did not say is that seeing something one way and then the other gives us a kind of measuring stick.

If we see a homeless man eating garbage, we might have a passing interest, but if we were aware that three weeks earlier he was as rich as Donald Trump, our interest would increase because of the stark contrast. "David and Goliath" is a story of this kind of contrast. So is "The Tortoise and the Hare" and "The Prince and the Pauper."

In each of these stories, one element defines another: large and small, slow and fast, rich and poor. Each condition increases the other's visibility. A giant cannot be a giant in a vacuum; he needs to be bigger than something, or he is no giant at all. In the same way, a story needs both light and dark if one is to tell it clearly and honestly.

POSTED FRIDAY, JULY 11, 2008

WATER SHORTAGE

SEVERAL YEARS AGO, I WROTE a script that had, as one of its elements, an army of ghosts. Everyone who read the screenplay swore it would sell for big money and that it was the best screenplay I had written up to that point. I was really proud of this script. I felt that I had nailed this story and its treatment.

But when I showed the screenplay to my agent at the time, he looked as if he had smelled sour milk. His comment was, "Dead people walking around—that's like Scooby-Doo. Don't they have dead people walking around?" He looked at me like I was a moron.

I was stunned. This was a fairly serious script. The ghosts were treated as a real threat. There was nothing there remotely like Scooby-Doo. (The cartoon, I mean. This was before the live-action movies.)

But let me put this in context for you: this was years before *The Sixth Sense,* and Hollywood hadn't yet rediscovered the power of the supernatural.

For a while, I was baffled as to why my screenplay made my agent think of a cartoon show. Then it hit me—he had no better reference for dead people walking around.

That's when I realized that imagination is like a reservoir: you can take out only what you have put in.

I grew up reading comics and watching *The Twilight Zone, Star Trek,* and *The Outer Limits.* I also had books full of art by fantasy artists like Frank Frazetta. My mind was full of fantastic images and stories. This was the reservoir from which I drew. All of these things I took in allowed me to create my own stories with their own realities.

My agent had many fewer images in his head from which to draw, so for him, dead people equaled Scooby-Doo. He had no other reference point.

I tell you this story because I have a hard time getting some of my students to watch older films or films outside a particular genre. But these things are ways of filling one's reservoir. This way, one understands that there can be many approaches to the same idea.

Look at Batman. There is the 1960s camp version. There is Tim Burton's version from the 1980s, which was inspired by Frank Miller's treatment of the character in *The Dark Knight* comic book. And there is the current film treatment by Christopher Nolan that I'm sure owes much to the Frank Miller/David Mazzucchelli take on the character in their comic book mini-series *Batman: Year One*. That book treated the character in a more realistic fashion than others had.

My point is that there are an infinite number of possibilities when it comes to how a story or character can be imagined. But your ideas are limited to your life experiences and the books, movies, television shows, music, and other art that you take in. So do what you can to experience more because, again, your imagination is a reservoir. The more you put in, the more you can take out later on.

POSTED MONDAY, JANUARY 22, 2007

PLEASE DON'T KILL THE ANIMALS

IN THE LAST COUPLE OF YEARS, several animated films have used animals as major characters. Now I am told by my friends in that business that the studios are looking to buck this trend. They feel that the audience is growing tired of watching animals. I find this baffling. Animal stories did not emerge in the world with the advent of computer-generated animation, and they will be with us long after we have moved on to some new technique.

We cannot help but see ourselves in the behavior and habits of animals. How many times have you heard someone say about his or her dog, "He thinks he's a person"? (A more accurate statement might be "I think my dog is a person.")

People constantly equate human and animal behaviors. They always have. It would not be out of the ordinary to hear a person say of someone, "That guy really squirrels away his money." In fact, here is a short list of such sayings:

- Those guys live like pigs.
- She watched me like a hawk.
- Men are dogs.
- Those guys are really butting heads.
- She eats like a bird.
- He's stubborn as a mule.

- She needs to come out of her shell.
- Those two go at it like a couple of rabbits.
- He's a leech.

Creative people have used animals in storytelling for all of human history. The ancient Greeks believed that by observing the way a beehive was organized and following that model, you could have a perfect society.

Many tribal peoples believe that one has an animal spirit guide, and by following that animal's lead, one might have an easier time at life. Tribal people also believe that we have an animal side to our natures, what Carl Jung called a "bush soul." So not only do we see ourselves in animals, but we also see the animal within ourselves.

But why do we use animals in stories, particularly? Because it is a way to look at ourselves with a little distance.

One of my favorite storytellers, Aesop, used animal stories to illuminate the nature of human beings. If the story of "The Tortoise and the Hare" were merely what the title suggests, few would remember the story. No, this is a story about people—people "dressed" for the story as a tortoise and a hare—but people nonetheless.

In the American South during the time of slavery, slaves told stories of the clever Brer (Brother) Rabbit. These were not stories of rabbits, foxes, and bears, but stories about people, designed to help them survive their cruel circumstances. They were stories about slaves outwitting their masters to get what they needed.

George Orwell's book *Animal Farm* uses that distance to reveal how people in power can abuse that power. And Art Spiegelman's brilliant graphic novel *Maus* uses cats as Nazis and mice as Jews to give the reader just enough emotional distance to see a Holocaust story through fresh eyes.

Less seriously, Daffy Duck provides the distance necessary to notice our greedy natures and laugh at ourselves.

If using animals to tell stories is just a trend, then it is a trend that stretches back to the beginning of human history. Maybe Hollywood needs to realize that the animals in their films did not write the stories they are telling. If people are tired of those, then it is not the animals that are to blame.

Posted Friday, October 13, 2006

Target Practice

The greater danger for most of us is not that our aim is too high and we miss it, but that it is too low and we reach it.

—Michelangelo

WHILE TEACHING A CLASS, I once mentioned that it wasn't just luck to repeatedly produce good work as a storyteller. I said that if it were being in the right place at the right time, you could not have people whose successes span decades such as Alfred Hitchcock or Billy Wilder.

One student scoffed and said, "Yeah, but that's Billy Wilder!" I could tell he had already decided what the limits of his talent were and was going to live within them.

That is not a helpful kind of self-appraisal. It allows one to make an excuse for substandard work, an excuse I have seen used a lot over the years. In the early '90s, I remember being in the studio of a popular comic book artist whose work could have been a little better. The artists who worked there didn't take their work very seriously. They wrote poor stories and made mediocre drawings.

When I asked why they didn't seem to care about the books' quality, one of them said, "It's just for kids." Does anyone think generation after generation would still be watching *Snow White and the Seven Dwarfs* if Walt Disney had ever said this to his artists? I don't think so. That attitude is just one of the many ways people excuse themselves from doing the hard work that it takes to produce something good.

Contrary to popular belief, quality work seldom comes easily for those who produce it. In fact, it is often most difficult for people at the top of their craft. (Thomas Mann said, "A writer is someone for whom writing is more difficult than it is for other people.") Professional writers are aiming high. They are looking at their heroes as competitors. Or they are aiming at a very specific idea or emotion, and they want to hit the bull's-eye. They are working at the limit of their abilities.

You have to always aim higher than you think you can reach.

The great Disney animator Glen Kean once told a friend of mine that he took on assignments only if he was afraid of them. He had to be unsure that he could pull it off. This is the kind of thinking that pushes one to do great work.

August Wilson and I were talking about this one day. He told me a story that illustrates the idea perfectly. He said that he was once working on a play as a submission to get into a playwriting workshop. A friend asked him what he was doing, and he said that he needed to write a play good enough for him to get into this workshop. The friend asked, "What are you doing that for? Why aren't you trying to write the best play ever written?"

August took his friend's point to heart. He now aimed to write the best play ever written. The result was *Ma Rainey's Black Bottom*—the first play of his ever produced on Broadway. August went on to win two Pulitzers for drama and a host of other awards, and he now has a theater on Broadway named for him. That is where pushing himself to the limit of his abilities got him.

So did he write the best play ever written? Let the critics argue that. The point is he tried, and in trying, he wrote a far better play than he would have done otherwise—and became one of the world's most admired playwrights.

Aim high—very high—higher than you think you might possibly reach, and you will produce work whose quality will surprise you.

Posted Tuesday, September 26, 2006

Hero Worship

"One must think like a hero to behave like a merely decent human being."
—*May Sarton*

WHAT HAPPENED TO HEROES in stories? In older films and stories, heroes were characters who made sacrifices. They were people who thought of others before themselves. At some point, we decided that this was unrealistic and that characters like a square-jawed Superman were too corny for us. We were more sophisticated than that—life is gray, not black and white. Bad guys and good guys went the way of the dodo. Nowadays, heroes are out for themselves. Maybe that is more realistic—but what lesson are we learning?

What people are forgetting about stories is why we tell them, and that "why" is very important. The "why" tells you how to tell a story. Almost all stories have a lesson at their core—sometimes a small lesson, sometimes profound, but almost always a lesson.

If you buy this idea, then what are heroes for? Why were they so goody-goody in the past? Heroes represent ideals to live up to. We learn from their example how we should try to behave. We see who we hope we will be when and if we are ever called on to be brave in the face of danger, be it physical or emotional. These examples are what we hope to imitate.

Stories are only a reflection of life. Flesh-and-blood heroes who are not fictional beings serve the same purpose—they have lived out ideals we hope to live up to. Look at Mahatma Gandhi, Mother Teresa, Albert Schweitzer, Martin Luther King, Jr.—very few of us can claim to be as self-sacrificing as they. And because we know what they did was right but not easy to do, we exalt these people.

A hero is measured by the size of his or her struggle. In many stories, a formidable villain shows us the hero's strength. But in others, a hero's internal struggle with what has been called a fatal flaw is the real obstacle to overcome. Giving a hero a weakness to overcome is what makes him or her like us. They are reluctant to do the right thing but do it anyway because it is the right thing to do.

How deep does this imitation go? In the 1930s, Clark Gable starred in a classic Frank Capra film called *It Happened One Night*. In a scene in that film, he undressed, and you could see that he wore no T-shirt. That year, the sales of T-shirts went down. Years later, in *Rebel Without a Cause*, James Dean wore a T-shirt as outerwear, and that became a fad.

These are just small examples of how we imitate our heroes. We also adopt their behaviors. We learn from their mindsets. As storytellers, we have a responsibility to show people who they could be if they face their demons and do the right thing. Sometimes people need a story to show them how they too can be heroes.

POSTED TUESDAY, SEPTEMBER 5, 2006

WHAT'S WRONG WITH EMOTIONS, ANYWAY?

WHEN WAS THE LAST TIME YOU FELT anything in the movie theater? I mean really felt something for the characters? Did you care who lived and who died? (I don't mean intellectually, but deep down in your gut.)

When a film is really working, people come out fired up. They are still giggling at the funny part or still worked up by the exciting part. Or they are still sad because of the melancholy part. More often than not, when I leave the theater, I don't hear people talking about the film at all. They just file out quietly unless they have something clever to say about what they have just seen. Just as often, they talk about getting lunch or dinner.

Part of what has happened is that academics have hijacked cinema. For them, emotional drama is cheap or manipulative. If it makes them cry, that's the worst kind of story.

But also, filmmakers have fallen in love with spectacle. These are the amazing special effects or stunts or scenery or sexy stars that create visceral, albeit superficial, emotions in the viewer. These cost a lot of money but are what I like to call "creatively inexpensive"—not hard to think up. And they have no lasting effect on the audience.

Aristotle put it like this: "The Spectacle has, indeed, an emotional attraction of its own, but, of all the parts, it is the least artistic, and connected least with the art of poetry [he means playwriting]. Fear and pity may be aroused by spectacular means; but they may also result from the inner structure of the piece, which is the better way, and indicates a superior poet. For the plot ought to be so constructed that, even without the aid of the eye, he who hears the tale told will thrill with horror and melt to pity at what takes place."

That's right. Thousands of years before computers, Aristotle in effect said, *Hey, don't go nuts with the special effects.*

We screenwriters have all but forgotten that our job is fundamentally to evoke emotional responses in the audience in order to make our point. Is this simply manipulation? No. This is the nature of drama. Making people feel things deeply requires more than cheap manipulation. This is, after all, what all art strives to do—to stir people.

Posted Tuesday, November 23, 2010

Isolation of Interest: More Thoughts on Learning

IF YOU EVER WANT TO GET BETTER at learning, become a teacher. You will see all of the things people do to stop themselves from learning. One thing we do that blocks us from learning is that we listen or read with an agenda. In magic, this is called isolation of interest.

Here is a story I have told before about a magician who was teaching a class on magic in Las Vegas. While at a craps table, he told the students that he would roll a seven. He passed the dice around to be examined to make sure they were normal dice. They passed inspection.

Then, as he said, the magician rolled a seven—to much amazement and applause. But he topped that by pointing out that the dice he passed around were red and the dice on the table were green.

By telling the spectators that he was going to roll a seven, he isolated their interest, and they never noticed him switch the dice. This kind of mono-focus makes us blind and deaf to all other things. Magicians know this very well. In cognitive science, it is known as selective attention.

If you listen to a teacher with an agenda, you will only listen for things relevant to that agenda and will miss or dismiss everything else.

I once taught a person who had studied geology. She told me that her professor once gave a test where he laid several rocks in a row on the table, and the students had to correctly identify them. No one noticed, but all of the rocks were of the same type.

When the professor revealed this fact, he told them, "The eye seldom sees what the mind does not anticipate."

The students had blinded themselves by looking only for what was different about the rocks; they could not see what was similar about them.

People can be so good at isolation of interest that I guarantee there is someone reading this blog post right now asking themselves what geology has to do with storytelling. They will fail to see any reason for me telling this story.

Another way people stop themselves from learning is to assume that they understand an idea at first blush. In the West, and in America in particular, we like to get things quickly. We think it makes us smart. This is reinforced by our educational systems. Malcolm Gladwell talks about this in his book *Outliers*.

I think this rush to understand things forces us to grasp ideas and concepts at only their most basic levels. We understand things on the surface but are unaware that there are layers and layers beneath that can take years to uncover. Zen practitioners understand the value of deep contemplation; there is no rush to "get it."

I have noticed that the people who actually don't "get it" are often the people who think they get it quickly. They are the ones who never look any deeper. But that is like looking at the surface of the ocean and believing that's all there is to it. There's a whole world underneath that you'll never see if you don't take the time to look.

I spoke with a woman not too long ago who was stuck on the ending for a short story she was working on. We talked for a while, and then I asked her to define what a story was, or at least what her definition of a story was. She stammered and could not answer the question.

I gave her my definition, which is very close to what the dictionary will tell you: a story is the telling of a series of events leading to a conclusion.

With that, she scoffed, as if to say, *Of course*. In fact, she said, "Sure, that's basic." Sure. It was so basic that when I asked her what a story was, she had no answer. But if she had this definition in her head, she would not have been stuck for an ending because that would have been where she was headed the entire time.

The reason she scoffed is why many people scoff at that kind of information—we have been taught that simple explanations must be flawed because they are not nuanced. But students are supposed to take this simple explanation, think about it, and make their own discoveries. I have learned that if you want to discover the profound, you should contemplate the mundane.

Take light, for instance. Light is all around us, and few of us think much about it. But great artists and thinkers have made profound discoveries from the study of light, including painters such as Vermeer and Rembrandt and scientists like Newton and Einstein.

Look, you don't have to agree with my definition of what a story is, but if you are a storyteller, you should start to consider how you might define it in the simplest terms for yourself. Don't be afraid to ask yourself the most basic of questions.

And as you study, try to be open to learning anything that comes. Don't limit yourself by isolating your interest.

Posted Friday, June 16, 2006

"The Humble Improve"

"The humble improve."
—*Wynton Marsalis*

THE SKETCHES IN THIS BLOG POST were done by my friend Derek Thompson, who works for Pixar and has sat in on two different seminars of mine. This was his way of taking notes.

STRUCTURE AND CHRONOLOGY HAVE NOTHING TO DO WITH ONE ANOTHER.
PROPOSAL. ARGUMENT. CONCLUSION. THOSE ARE YOUR 3 ACTS.
EXIT
ANOTHER 3 ACT STRUCTURE
• TELL THEM WHAT YOU'RE GOING TO TELL THEM.
• TELL THEM.
• TELL THEM WHAT YOU TOLD THEM.
"UH OH" MOMENT
THE ARMATURE QUESTION SHOULD BE ANSWERED BY THE DRAMA THAT FOLLOWS.
READ AESOP.
AIM HIGH.

A few months ago, I had the privilege of teaching a seminar at Pixar. Anyone who knows me knows that there are few modern storytellers I respect as much as those at Pixar. They are the best.

I was as nervous as I have ever been in my life. I worship these people. You think I'm kidding, but I cannot express here just how highly I regard their work. At one point while speaking, I thought I might pass out, my head was spinning so fast.

All of the tension I was feeling was self-generated, by the way. The people at Pixar could not have been nicer. They were sweet, generous, humble people. Not one person swaggered with pride or puffed their chest out. These were the people who made *Toy Story* and *Toy Story 2*; *A Bug's Life*; *Monsters, Inc.*; *The Incredibles*; and (my personal favorite) *Finding Nemo*, and they walked with their feet planted firmly on the ground. And the strangest thing of all—they wanted to hear what I had to say about story construction.

A friend of mine used to say after dispensing advice, "But what do I know? I'm just some guy." That's the way I felt—I'm just some guy. But they listened to me to see just what I had to teach them. As I said before, these are humble people. This is a key element to their success.

KNOW WHERE YOU ARE GOING.
THERE'S ALWAYS A POINT WHERE A CHARACTER GOES TO HELL. HOPEFULLY IT'S THEIR OWN PERSONAL HELL.
IF YOU CAN FIGURE OUT THE LAST PLACE YOUR CHARACTER WANTS TO BE, AND YOU PUT THEM THERE...
CLONES.
Read "IMPRO" Keith Johnston
WHEN YOU CONVEY AN INTELLECTUAL IDEA EMOTIONALLY, THAT'S DRAMA.
WHAT COULD SHOULD OR MIGHT HAPPEN TO YOUR CHARACTER IF THEY TOOK ANOTHER PATH.

As I've mentioned before, I was lucky enough to become friends with acclaimed playwright August Wilson a few years before he died. One day shortly after we met, I mentioned the story structure class that I teach, and he said that he should take it. I was blown away. I said, "You have two Pulitzers to my zero. Why would you want to take my class?" He told me a story about a guy he knew who had once met the great jazz saxophonist John Coltrane. The man sheepishly mentioned to Coltrane that he too played the saxophone. Coltrane's response was, "What can you teach me?" August wanted to know what I could teach him. In fact, I was once on my cell phone, and August approached and hovered around until I got off the phone. He then asked me for advice on his new play. I told him what I thought he should do, and he took notes and listened. The man knew that he didn't have all the answers and wasn't afraid to seek them out. This was a man at the top of his field who showed the same dedication to continued learning that I would later witness at Pixar.

1-21-06
INVISIBLE INK WORKSHOP
BRIAN SAYS PICK 5 OF YOUR FAVORITE MOVIES : (NO NEED TO IMPRESS.)
KING KONG
JAWS
THE EMPIRE STRIKES BACK
ALIENS
GHOSTBUSTERS
THE SEVEN STEPS OF A BETTER STORY
① ONCE UPON A TIME...
② ...AND EVERY DAY...
③ ...UNTIL ONE DAY...
④ ...AND BECAUSE OF THIS...
⑤ ...AND BECAUSE OF THIS...
⑥ ...UNTIL FINALLY...
⑦ ...AND EVER SINCE THAT DAY...

I have seen over and over again that the best people are humble before their craft and don't lean on their past successes. They are hungry for knowledge and know that they will never reach that elusive goal of knowing everything. One must always move toward the horizon even though the horizon keeps its distance.

POSTED FRIDAY, MAY 26, 2006

THE AMAZING DISAPPEARING FIRST ACT

"Learn the fundamentals of the game and stick to them."
—*Jack Nicklaus*

I HATE TO COME BACK to the whole three-act thing, but I find again and again that people are not adhering to it. My belief is that the lack of strong first acts in films in recent years has much to do with the steady decline in movie attendance. No first act equals no emotional involvement.

I think I mentioned before that I have been studying magic. There are many benefits for storytellers who study magic, one of which is the importance of the first act. Even the simplest magic trick uses three-act structure. In his book *Magic Book,* Milbourne Christopher puts it this way: "The magician can assume nothing. Unless an audience has been led to believe that a closed hand holds a coin, they will not be amazed when it is shown to be empty."

He's talking about having a clear first act.

This idea of being clear often frightens my students. They don't want to point out the obvious. But what is obvious to them may not be so obvious to the audience.

Milbourne continues, "If they are not aware that an object is green, they will not be astonished when the color changes to red. My friend [magician] Paul Ebling illustrated this point during a demonstration of gambling techniques. He passed around a pair of unprepared dice with white spots for examination. Then he announced he would shake the dice and roll a seven. The seven came up as promised. This was a far more remarkable feat than the spectators realized. Until Paul reminded them that the dice that they examined had been green, no one had noticed that the dice on the table were red."

People notice only what you tell them to notice. If you want to involve them, be obvious about what you want them to notice. Magicians understand this, but over the years, I have seen a decline in the understanding and importance of a strong first act in storytelling. The tendency is to want to get to the meat of a story because that's where all the fun happens.

I often use jokes as examples because they are little stories. Everyone knows the importance of a strong first act when they are telling a joke. And the listener knows that everything they are being told will help them understand the punch line of the joke. A listener would never say, "Just skip all of that crap and get to the ending." And joke-tellers know that act one is so important that when they are in the middle of a joke and have forgotten something, they will be sure to go back and fill in the missing information. "Oh, wait, I forgot to say that the guy has a duck in his pants."

But first acts are all but disappearing from films. There is almost no time spent setting up the characters and the world they inhabit before the inciting incident. They deprive the audience of any emotional involvement. Imagine a magician's opening move being that he takes a card randomly out of a deck and asks triumphantly, "Is this your card?" Not much of a trick. With no setup, there is no trick. No emotional involvement. Same with stories.

Don't be afraid to take the time it takes to give your audience all they need to know in order to become gripped by your story.

Posted Monday, May 15, 2006

The Other Side of the Roller Coaster

AT THIS TIME OF THE YEAR, the studios put out their big movies, also called their "tentpole" films. Their marketers will call these "nonstop roller coaster rides!" *Roller coaster* is the term that they use to describe films with relentless action. They promise all the thrills, chills, twists, and turns of the tallest roller coaster at Magic Mountain or Great America or wherever.

Why are these movies almost always a letdown? Shouldn't action scene after action scene be exciting?

Well, ask yourself, what is the scariest part of the roller coaster? The three-story drop? The corkscrew twist? The big loop? Probably not.

Anticipation is almost always the thing that scares us the most. It is the calm before the storm that is the scariest. Imagine yourself in line to go on the world's biggest and most frightening coaster—the Widowmaker or something. Imagine the signs warning that those with weak hearts or back problems and pregnant women should not ride. Imagine seeing others on the ride before you. They scream in abject terror. All of this is all part of the experience—the anticipation. Imagine watching the cars maneuver through the loops, twists, and spills of the coaster. You watch as people exit the ride, some exhilarated, others shaken and unstable. Some are just plain ill, to put it nicely.

Finally, it's your turn. You are ushered into your seat where you are strapped in. The safety bar comes down across your midsection.

Ironically, the safety equipment makes you feel even more nervous. You ask yourself, *How bad is this thing if they need all of this stuff to keep me safe?*

With a jolt, your car starts to move. The butterflies in your gut are flapping like crazy. The first leg on the track is level. Then you see it. The track ahead stretches up and up and up. Your car starts to ascend. Click, click, click goes the chain that carries your car ever upward. It seems to take forever to reach the top. You wonder again just how bad the drop will be when you crest this hill.

Then there is that sweet, terrifying, white-knuckle moment when at long last you reach the top. Here it comes.

The drop itself is more of a release of built-up tension. But these precious moments of anticipation are all part of what makes a roller coaster scary. It is not wall-to-wall action alone that fills you with delicious anxiety but the quiet moments as well. They are the yin and yang of the experience.

Movies that wish to duplicate this feeling often leave out half of the experience. They have almost no quiet moments.

Take a film like *Aliens*. Now, here is a film that most people remember as nonstop action, but there are many moments of quiet, many moments that allow the audience to anticipate how bad things are going to get for the characters in the film.

So many filmmakers now want to cut right to the chase, the big explosion, the monster, the running and jumping, the firefight, the murder. There is no click, click, click as the tension builds.

They make the mistake of thinking that because the screams come when the monster shows up, only the monster is scary. They forget about the other part of the roller coaster ride. It's the same as thinking that the best part of a joke is the punch line, as if the setup did not contribute to the joke. Why not a joke with no setup, just one punch line after another? Wouldn't that be the funniest thing ever? Wall-to-wall punch lines!

It sounds ridiculous, but it is the same thing as wall-to-wall action. It's the same "just the good parts" philosophy.

No, just as the setup is an important part of a joke, so are the quiet moments of anticipation part of an action sequence. You cannot have one without the other.

So this summer when you emerge from the theater a little disappointed that you were not more thrilled by the action, ask yourself if the filmmakers bothered to remember that a roller coaster goes both up and down. Chances are they did not.

Posted Friday, April 16, 2010

This Is Not a Pipe: The Value of Research

A PLAYWRIGHT ONCE TOLD ME that I should write a book about how to do research. Until she said this, I had no idea I was any good at it. But I have noticed that people will often comment on a feeling of authenticity in my work, and if that is true at all, it is due to research.

I divide research into two kinds: soft research and hard research. Hard research is what most of us do. This is research for factual data, things such as when the Spanish-American War was and why it was fought. Or finding out how tall George Washington was. Or who is buried in Grant's Tomb.

These are just hard facts, easily looked up in a book or on the Internet. But there is another kind of research that I find even more valuable—soft research.

Back when I was a teenager trying to learn my trade, I read an interview with Lawrence Kasdan just after *Raiders of the Lost Ark* came out. I was obsessed with *Raiders* and Kasdan. And because he had written the screenplays for both *Raiders* and *The Empire Strikes Back,* I wanted to read anything he had to say. I would follow his advice to the letter.

Well, in this interview, Kasdan said that one of the things he did when doing research for *Raiders* was read books and see movies that came out the year that *Raiders* took place. That made sense to me. This is why there is an authentic voice to the piece. It feels very much like something from the 1930s.

Kasdan's approach is a perfect example of soft research. This kind of information goes beyond facts. It gets to the feeling of things—the intangible. And these things can make their way into your story or art or whatever in ways you could never predict.

When you are engaged in soft research, you should do it without a goal. You should just be open to taking in information. Take everything in.

When the guys at Pixar were making *Finding Nemo,* they got certified to scuba dive. This gave them the experience they needed to make their film feel as if it were taking place in an actual natural environment.

I was once working with animation students on a project that took place in the woods. I could not convince them to go spend time in the woods to soak up the environment. They thought looking at pictures of trees on the Internet was the same thing as going into the woods and looking at real trees. It isn't.

There are things those students could have learned in the woods that they never could learn from books or the Internet. Bruce Lee said, "If you want to learn to swim, jump into the water. On dry land no frame of mind is ever going to help you."

As much as possible, you want to "get in the water." Soft research puts you in the water. When you are immersed in the world you want to recreate, you will have a much easier time doing so.

If I am writing a piece that takes place in the past, I will see films, read books, listen to music, watch television shows, listen to radio shows, watch talk shows, and look at art made during that time. I find that comic strips are good because what people laugh at tells you a lot about what they were feeling at the time. They really tell you about what people were serious about.

Hard research is the key to making your work accurate, but soft research is the key to making your work *feel* accurate.

POSTED TUESDAY, MAY 4, 2010

TOO MUCH OF A GOOD THING: THE PITFALLS OF RESEARCH

"If your work shows, you're in trouble."
—*Chuck Jones*

I WAS ONCE WRITING A SCRIPT on a particular topic, and as part of my research, I was reading the *For Dummies* book on this subject. Someone saw me reading this book and scoffed. I took that to mean that I should have been reading a more "serious" book on the subject. Why? To avoid embarrassment? I wasn't trying to impress anyone. I was trying to learn enough about my subject to write about it.

Don't fall into the trap of trying to impress others with your research. This can rear its ugly head in the writing itself. You want to show off all of the work you did. But this only takes the focus away from your story and characters and puts the focus on the writer. This kind of storytelling pulls people out of the story rather than sucking them in.

The more people are emotionally invested in your story, the more effective it will be. Don't show your work.

Another trap of research is procrastination. Writers love to procrastinate. If procrastination were an Olympic event, writers would win the gold medal every time. Research is perfect for writers because they can fool themselves into thinking that they are working. We writers can research a subject for years and make ourselves believe that we are working. Now, some subjects really do take years to research. They really do. So how do you know when you are finished?

The trick I use is that when I start to feel as if I have read most of the things more than once, I am finished. In other words, when information is repeated by several sources, I quit my research.

Another thing that can happen is that research sparks other ideas. You may start with one idea and, upon researching the subject, discover other things you could tell stories about. Now you can't decide what to do. This is just another form of procrastination.

What you do is make a decision. You can always tell those other stories. Just pick one and tell it. There will more than likely be one that pulls you more than the others. You may be afraid of this idea because it may be more challenging, but that's exactly why you should choose it.

OK, time for me to get back to work. When I want to procrastinate, I write a blog post.

Posted Thursday, May 20, 2010

Life: The Other Kind of Research

"I'm trying to take culture and put it onstage, demonstrate it is capable of sustaining you. There is no idea that can't be contained by life: Asian life, European life, certainly Black life. My plays are about love, honor, duty, betrayal—things humans have written about since the beginning of time."

—*August Wilson*

AUGUST WILSON WAS FOND OF SAYING that he didn't do research. When I asked him about it, he said, "I figure if they had horse-drawn milk wagons when I was coming up in the fifties then they had them in the twenties."

The truth is, August researched all the time. He read a lot, for one. But he also spent a ton of time with people, all kinds of people. People fascinated him. And he wasn't quick to judge them; he was far more interested in what made them tick. He wanted to know why people did what they did, or how people got to be who they were.

If you are a storyteller, your job is to observe and report on human behavior—the world is your classroom. You have to be a keen observer of human behavior. And the great thing about humans is that they are everywhere. It is safe to assume that you see and interact with a human being almost every day.

No matter what you are telling stories about, at their core will be human emotions and motivations. You can get many details wrong, but if your characters don't behave as people do in real life, all the other research in the world will not help you. You have to learn how to "see" people.

I would say that "seeing" is at least as important as "doing" when it comes to art. Art is about both how *you* see and what *you* see. When someone does something you would never do or can't understand, ask yourself why. You have to do this with clarity and without judgment. This is the hardest part of observation—to do it without judgment.

Why is it important not to judge your characters? Because characters who are judged by the storyteller tend to be caricatures rather than characters—cutouts rather than real people. Over the years, I have met many writers who are quick to judge but few who strive for understanding. And good story writing is honest—sometimes painfully so.

The best place to look is inside yourself. But not at the parts of yourself that you think are great. No, you must find those things about yourself that you'd rather not look at. The things you keep in the dark. That's where you mine the real dramatic gold. That's where the humanity is.

Look at others, look at yourself—find the humanity in both. That's how you write something that matters.

Posted Wednesday, May 10, 2006

Inkblot Cinema

A WHILE AGO, I HAD A TALK with a musician friend of mine. He told me that he had gone to see a modern classical concert. He said that it was an awful cacophony and asked, "What happened to the art of communication?" I thought that was a very good question, one I have often wondered about myself.

I saw a documentary on television about the phenomenon of genius, and in it they said that it was a Western concept that someone might be so smart that they could not be understood. Sometimes when an artist fails to communicate with his or her audience, the audience is blamed for not understanding. This is an easy out. It's too convenient to put the onus for communication on the listener. I have never been sure where the skill lies in confusing one's audience. Any five-year-old can be unclear.

Unfortunately, storytellers who communicate clearly are often considered juvenile or pedestrian, such as Hitchcock and Spielberg. When Hitchcock was making films, the intelligentsia treated him much the way Spielberg is treated now. His films were seen simply as crowd-pleasers. Yet both put so much attention on communicating with their audiences that their very names have become synonymous with film itself.

When I talk to people about communication in art, they often say that they don't want to be handed everything; they want to figure things out for themselves. Artists who think this way often create confusing art. This is a common trait of intellectuals. The smarter people are, the more they like art that is obscure and difficult to understand.

Yet the smarter someone is, the easier they are to fool. Magic, for instance, depends on the viewer's ability to put together pieces of information and draw the most logical conclusion. If a magician takes a coin and transfers it from one hand to another, and then the coin is made to disappear, chances are the coin never left the first hand.

But because by the time we are adults we have all seen objects pass from one hand to another countless times, we assume it has happened. I call this gap-closing, and smart people are really good at it. A professional magician friend of mine confirmed my observation that scientists and skeptics are the easiest to fool.

Gap-closing also happens when someone tells a joke. A joke is just a story with a part missing; that missing piece is supplied by the listener. When they make the connection, they laugh. In fact, kids will often exclaim, "I get it!" They have pieced the clues together and closed the gap. With a well-constructed joke, we all close the same gap; everyone draws the same conclusion.

If the gap is too close, as in the case of a pun, people often don't think much of it. The further the gap, the funnier the joke. But there is a limit. Everyone knows that if you have to explain it, it isn't funny. It often means that the gap is too great and most people can't close it, or that people are drawing different conclusions trying to close it.

I wish people held art to the same high standards they hold jokes to: if you have to explain it, it isn't working. Smart people will often fill in the gap with something that seems to make sense, but if you ask these gap-closers what they "got," they will all say something different. I call this "inkblot art," or when I'm talking about film, "inkblot cinema." With inkblot cinema, people see what they want to see. They like what they see because they made it up themselves. But often they have done to themselves what the magician does; they have fooled themselves into seeing something that is not there. Like a skillful magician or comedian, a good storyteller can use this gap-closing to his or her advantage. Hitchcock called it "pure cinema." He let the audience close gaps all the time.

In *Frenzy*, Hitchcock shows us a brutal murder. Later in the film, he shows the killer disappearing into an apartment with a young woman. As the killer closes the door, he uses the exact words he used just before he committed the earlier murder. Then he keeps the viewer outside the door to imagine what is happening on the other side. Everyone is closing the gap like crazy, but we are all closing the same one. We all know a brutal murder is taking place on the other side of the door.

Billy Wilder said, "Let the audience add up two plus two. They'll love you forever." Just make sure you have communicated well enough that the audience knows the answer is four. Don't hide behind your inability to be clear or rely on the ability of your audience to make up something where there is nothing.

Bring back the art of communication.

Posted Monday, October 4, 2010

A Few Thoughts on Learning

"Being ignorant is not so much a shame, as being unwilling to learn."

—*Benjamin Franklin*

BEFORE I START THIS BLOG POST, I will warn you that there is a little bit of swearing and a bit of imagery that may be slightly off-putting to some. But I think the lesson of this post is an important one and worth the risk of offending.

I am often taken aback by students and others I talk to who say they want to learn about something but then reject information about their subject of interest.

An aspiring screenwriter once approached me. She told me she was looking for the secret to engaging an audience. She said that there must be a way to hold an audience spellbound and keep their attention. She spoke with the passion of a person on a quest for the secret to the universe. She went on for a while, wondering aloud if there was some trick or technique that might help her engage an audience in this way.

I told her that she should read interviews with Alfred Hitchcock because he was quite articulate about how to involve an audience in your story.

The woman scoffed and said, "I don't like Hitchcock's movies, so I don't care what he said."

My head still spins when I think about it. Hitchcock had a fifty-year career because he knew how to play an audience like a fiddle. His nickname is Master of Suspense. The man has a list of classics as long as my arm, and this would-be screenwriter blew him off like a one-hit wonder.

The truth is she didn't want the answer to her question; she wanted to be on her intellectual quest. For her, pondering this "unanswerable" question was its own reward.

One of the other things people will say to me is that they'd like to take my class just to learn screenwriting. They will say that they already know how to write because they write poetry or something.

They have already made the assumption that they aren't learning a new craft but merely learning a few technical details particular to screenwriting. This is like a biologist deciding that he can build a rocket ship because he is a scientist. How different can it be?

I see this all the time. People dismiss new information with confidence, even cockiness, born of ignorance.

I was once introduced to the friend of a good friend of mine. Both of these people are trained martial artists. This woman, during our chance meeting on the street, mentioned that she was creating her very own martial art. This sounded ridiculous to me, and I wondered just who she thought she was.

When she and my friend were finished visiting, we said our nice-to-meet-yous, and she walked off.

As soon as she was gone, my friend turned to me and said that this woman was the best martial artist he had ever seen—she knew many martial arts and was a champion in them. Whenever she wanted to learn a new form, she never told her teacher who she was. She would take the class as if she were a beginner. She learned the basics and worked her way to the top.

This is a person who can put her ego aside in order to learn something new. Impressive.

More than once, I have finished teaching a class and students have excitedly told me how much they learned. And they say that they want to learn more. If I give them a list of movies to watch, they often point out the films that they have already seen and tell me that they don't need to see those. Or they will watch some of the films and report back on which ones they didn't like.

Understand that after the class, they tell me how much I changed the way they "see" stories, and yet they blow off the very thing I know will help them learn more: patient study.

First, they shouldn't refuse to watch a film they have already seen, because now they are looking at it with new eyes. They know more than they knew when they saw it before. And secondly, if they don't like a film on my list, what they should do is ask themselves why I thought they could learn from it.

I had one student who watched and didn't like Billy Wilder's *The Apartment*. He had no idea why I thought it was good. But you know what he did? He watched it again. And again. And again. Until he saw what I saw. Now he loves the film and sees the craftsmanship that was invisible to him before. He did the very same thing with Hitchcock's *Rear Window*. He now loves that film as well. And he has learned how to be a better storyteller.

The following story is a little vulgar but worth telling to make my point.

I used to know a man from a West African village. We once talked about his manhood initiation ritual. He said to me in his thick accent, "In my village, when you are a boy in manhood training, you must go take a *sheet* in the woods." He paused. "Then you sit all day and you watch your sheet." In case you are at all confused, "sheet" was his mispronunciation of another word that is more graphic in nature. He paused for a long while. I had no idea what he was getting at. Then he said, "Then you see *everything* that depends on your sheet."

I realized that the village boys learn from this exercise their vital connection to the rest of the living world. This is a profound lesson to emerge from such a seemingly pointless act.

Remember that sometimes when someone is trying to teach you something new, your job is not to judge what he or she asks you to do, but to fully understand why you should do it.

If you do this, you may be surprised by what you have allowed yourself to learn.

Posted Wednesday, January 4, 2006

We Live in the Dark Ages

THESE ARE THE DARK TIMES. This is, in my opinion, the worst time in the history of cinema. This trend toward bad films began around 1980. When I say this to friends, they often say that I just like old movies and that bad films have always been made. They are correct that bad films have always been produced, but there also used to be a lot more good films and more than a few masterpieces. I offer as proof of my point that when I was a kid, people would go to the movies and expect them to be good and be disappointed when they were bad. Now people go the movies expecting them to be bad and are surprised when they are good. High praise for a film nowadays is someone saying, "It wasn't as bad as I thought it would be." How many times have you heard this or said it yourself?

Many things contribute to this trend, but at the top of my list is the death of the first act. The great screenwriter and director Billy Wilder said, "If you have a problem with the third act, the real problem is in the first act."

Act one is of the utmost importance to storytelling and is all but forgotten by modern storytellers.

What is act one? It tells the audience what the story will be about. Sounds easy enough, but people still choose not to write one because it isn't the meat of a story. Storytellers are impatient and want to get to the "good part" as fast as possible.

Sounds smart, right? But it isn't. The "good part" of a joke is the punch line, so I'll just give you the good part of a joke: The old man from the faraway country was taken aback and was silent for a long time. As he got up to leave the subway train, he leaned over to the priest and said, "Mister, maybe you should wear your pants backwards."

Not that funny? But that's the funny part. It doesn't work because there is no context. Act one provides the context for a story. Everything that happens in the rest of the story somehow relates to act one. A well-crafted act one can make or break a story.

If you have read the installments of this blog that deal with armature, you will be familiar with this: Tell them what you're going to tell them. Tell them. Tell them what you told them.

That is really the best definition for the three acts I have ever seen. Today we are dealing with the "tell them what you are going to tell them" part. That is act one. If your story's point is that even a good man can be corrupted by power, then your first act shows a good man without power. You must show that he is squeaky clean and even show him in a situation where he could be corrupt and is not.

This is also where you let the audience know "the outer boundaries" of the reality of the story. *E.T.* starts with E.T., not Elliot. Now the audience knows to expect aliens in this story. *It's a Wonderful Life* starts with two angels talking so that the audience knows to expect a supernatural element. This all falls under "tell them what you are going to tell them." The film *Raiders of the Lost Ark* begins with a big action sequence before we end up in Professor Indiana Jones' classroom. We know there is more action coming because we got an outer boundaries scene. The storytellers told us what was to come.

The primary job of a storyteller is to communicate, and a strong first act will help you do that.

WEDNESDAY, JANUARY 4, 2006

WE LIVE IN THE DARK AGES, PART 2

THE MORE I TALK ABOUT AND TEACH structure, the more I see that people have a fundamental misunderstanding about what it really is. Story structure is not an edict from on high that says, "One must tell stories like this!" It is more basic than that—it is the way people naturally tell stories. Storytelling is as natural to human beings as language itself.

Here are the three parts of drama: proposal, argument, conclusion.

Each of these parts represents an act in a three-act structure. You use this structure every day. We all do.

A story is the telling or retelling of a series of events leading to a conclusion. People have an instinct for story—we know what one is, and we know all the rules. Our intellect fools us into thinking that it can be many things. But we know that isn't true in life.

Here's how people tell stories. This is from a book I was reading about hypnosis called *Self Hypnosis: The Technique and Its Use in Daily Living* by Leslie M. LeCron. LeCron wanted to make a point about how diverting your attention away from pain can lessen the pain. This is how it appears in the book:

A lesson in psychology from a veterinarian. My daughter once owned a cat which I took to a vet for shots, two of which are given a week apart. The assistant took the kitten on the first visit. He placed the kitten on the table and reached for the syringe. The animal sensed something unpleasant was about to happen and began to struggle and yowl. The assistant asked me to help hold the cat. I grasped its legs while he held its head with one hand and inserted the needle in its back with the other. As he gave the injection the kitten wailed loudly in pain.

The next week the older veterinarian took it. As I placed it on the table I asked if he wanted me to help hold it. "Oh no," he answered, "that's not necessary." Putting his hand behind the kitten's head he began to bump its nose up and down on the table while he reached for the syringe with his other hand. Deftly inserting the needle, he gave the injection with the kitten not even whimpering. It was too busy wondering what was happening to its nose to feel pain.

This is the way we all use stories every day. The man telling the story knew instinctively about three-act structure. He used clone characters for comparison. He never strayed from his point. And we understand his point clearly. This is how people talk. That is why stories are the way they are. The structure is natural for us. The teller of this story stated his proposal as "A Lesson from a Veterinarian." He then went on to prove, or argue, his point, and he concluded by summing up his meaning. Take any part away from this story and it becomes unclear.

I often hear the argument that a good story is layered and has many points, and that "my way" is too simplistic. Looking again at the veterinarian story, even though the writer had one point and made it, there are other things to be learned from it as well. He could use the same story to talk about the wisdom of age versus the inexperience of youth, for instance. A story told clearly and precisely will be full of wisdom without much effort by you to insert it.

Since such films as *Pulp Fiction* and *Memento,* people have talked a lot about how these movies "redefined" structure because they were told out of sequence. People use them as evidence that those "rules" about structure are breakable. This is only proof to me that people do not understand structure. In real life, we tell stories out of sequence all the time. We might say, "I got fired from my job today." Then we might follow by saying, "So my boss walks up to me..." This is telling a story out of sequence, and people do it all the time. All of these "rules" can be observed every day in real life.

Posted Wednesday, January 11, 2006

The Strange Case of Sherman Alexie

I WAS ONCE ASKED TO GIVE A TALK about storytelling to a convention of high school media students with Native American writer Sherman Alexie. The problem was no one told Sherman, so he spoke the entire time. That worked out perfectly for me because I got a great story out of it.

Sherman doesn't believe in formalized story structure; he believes that it is a Hollywood construct. He began his presentation by saying that there was no such thing as three-act structure and no such thing as a happy ending. He said that life doesn't work out that neatly. He then went on to say that he could not teach the students to write, but he could tell them how he became a writer. He said that when he was a kid on the reservation, he was sick most of the time, so he spent most of his time reading. He read every book in the reservation library, and when he was done, he started over and reread them. Most of the people he interacted with were doctors and health care professionals, so he wanted to be a pediatrician when he grew up.

When he was old enough, he enrolled in college and began taking pre-med anatomy classes. In pre-med anatomy classes, students must work with actual corpses. On the first day of class, a cadaver was unveiled and Sherman fainted. He thought that maybe he should drop the class. His teacher convinced him to stay. Another day while he was working on a body, it farted and Sherman fainted. He decided again that he should quit but once again was persuaded to stay. The third time he fainted while working on a body, he finally decided to drop the class.

He then had a hole in his schedule and didn't know what to do or what the future held for him. He saw that there was a poetry class, and he had always liked poetry, so he signed up for the class.

Sherman said that he had never read poetry by an Indian before. He didn't even know Indians wrote poetry. He had only read poems by dead white people. The professor showed Sherman wonderful poems written by people who shared his background. This was great.

At one point, the students were asked to write poems and give them to the other students to take home, read, and evaluate. The next day, Sherman was one of the first to arrive to class. As he sat there, a female classmate came in and began to talk to Sherman and praise him for his poem. She went on and on about how much she liked it. Then another woman chimed in with her gushing praise, and another and another. Soon, he was surrounded by women telling him how good he was. "That," he said, "is how I became a writer."

What struck me about this story was that Sherman preceded it with the statement that there was no such thing as three-act structure and no such thing as a happy ending. This was not reflective of real life, he said. Then he told a story from his real life that had three acts and a happy ending. If you go back and look, I'm sure you'll be able to identify the acts.

Posted Thursday, March 23, 2006

Paddy Chayefsky's Dead

STARTING SOMETIME IN THE 1980S, film directors became art directors. The look of a film became more important than any other aspect of the film. So all the guys who cared more about style than substance have been touted as geniuses. It is not unusual nowadays to hear a critic wax poetic about the look of a film regardless of its narrative substance. Not to pick on *Memoirs of a Geisha,* but all anyone could say about it was that it was beautiful. One hears that a lot these days.

Many of my friends think I like old films because they are old. This is not so. I like older films and filmmakers because they were better. The people who wrote and directed films during Hollywood's Golden Age and just following were a hundred times smarter than almost anyone doing the job now. There are some exceptions like Alexander Payne and Jim Taylor, Frank Darabont, John Lasseter, Andrew Stanton, Steven Zaillian, and a few others. But for the most part, the people who get to make films today have a knowledge of film history that goes all the way back to Michael Jackson's "Thriller" video. They also have little or no knowledge of the storyteller's craft.

Movies are getting worse and worse. Box office is down for the third year in a row. Movies cost ten bucks, and we, the audience, get less for our money. Back when a person could go to the movies for the amount of the loose change in their pockets, they got a newsreel, a short subject and/or cartoon, and a great movie. Sometimes you could see a live vaudeville act called a "cooler" because it was put on between screenings while the projector cooled. Imagine seeing a hilarious new Bugs Bunny cartoon followed by *Casablanca* or *The Maltese Falcon*. Today, we pay a lot more for a whole lot less.

Hollywood blames the emergence of new media for the drop in ticket sales. That's an easy scapegoat that takes the responsibility off them. One of the most profitable times for film was during the Great Depression. You don't think people had other things they could spend their money on? Things like rent and food? They did. But they went to the movies anyway. Guess why? They were entertained.

The storytellers of past generations just plain knew more about their craft than the current crop. They knew that there is a history of storytelling that goes back as far as humanity. They knew that they had to honor that history and the lessons learned from those who had come before. They also made astute observations about audiences and their reactions.

You can test this theory of mine by picking a current top filmmaker and reading an interview with them to see how much insight they have; then read an older interview with Billy Wilder, Alfred Hitchcock, John Huston, Frank Capra, or Paddy Chayefsky. In these older interviews, you will find information that will help you become a better storyteller. These guys have the keys to the kingdom. They are the keepers of knowledge that is all but lost to the ages.

Two of the best books to read are *Hitchcock Truffaut,* which is an extended interview with Hitchcock by filmmaker Francois Truffaut, and Paddy Chayefsky's *The Collected Works of Paddy Chayefsky: The Television Plays*. This book is great. The plays themselves are good, but the essays that follow each play are even better. Here you will read just how the stories were put together. It is one of the best books about story construction I have ever read. It's like a mini film school. After you read these books, most of the modern filmmakers will sound like troglodytes.

So next time you want to go the movies and see a good show, go to the cemetery instead and watch Alfred Hitchcock and Paddy Chayefsky spinning in their graves over what has happened to their craft. I'm sure that will be a much more entertaining show than whatever they are showing at the multiplex.

Posted Monday, November 1, 2010

A Lesson from Paddy Chayefsky

"When you ask a writer what their story's about and they give you plot, you're in trouble."
—*a paraphrased quote by director Sydney Pollack*

IN THE 1950S, PADDY CHAYEFSKY made a huge splash with a teleplay he wrote called *Marty*. *Marty* went on to become a hit movie and an Academy Award winner.

Chayefsky wrote many things of note in television, film, and theater. He was a writer's writer (he's Neil Simon's favorite author) who was known for writing smart material that also connected with an audience. The man had an effect on art and culture that is still felt today.

If you want to know just how smart he is, buy a copy of *The Collected Works of Paddy Chayefsky: The Television Plays,* where he breaks down his working method. You'll learn a ton.

Back in 1980, I was a kid who was just learning the name Chayefsky. I would often hear people the generation ahead of me quote lines from *Marty*: "What do you wanna to do?" "I dunno…what do you wanna to do?" You'll have to see the film, but these were very famous lines.

As a fifteen-year-old, I had not yet seen *Marty* or even Chayefsky's other classic film, *Network*. But 1980 saw the release of a film he had written called *Altered States*. This movie blew my little teenage mind. I had never seen anything quite like it. (That was the year I spent most of my movie money on *The Empire Strikes Back* and decided I should mix it up a little.)

What floored me about *Altered States* was how real it seemed to me. It may look dated to younger eyes, but at the time, it looked and felt much like the real world. This was a Chayefsky trademark. That's why he could make a line like "What do you wanna do?" famous.

In the film, a scientist seeks the ultimate truth (by ingesting hallucinogenic drugs while inside an isolation chamber) and taps into some primal force that causes him to regress to a protohuman form.

There are also a bunch of lame acid-trip montages that Chayefsky hated so much, he took his name off the film as screenwriter. They were lame then, and they don't age well at all.

But the rest of the story really intrigued me, so I decided to read up on this famous writer. I came across an interview where he said that *Altered States* was really a love story. What? This made no sense to me. So I saw the film over and over, trying to see what he was talking about.

When I had seen the film enough to look past the cool effects and concept, I could see the story clearly. It is about a man who cannot love and, in the end, learns to love and learns the value of love. This was Chayefsky's reason to tell the story.

This changed everything for me. I learned that no matter what a story looked like on the outside, no matter how cool the concept, there should be a human story at its core.

So when I saw *Jaws,* I knew it wasn't about a shark but about a man learning to face his fear, and through facing it, he conquered it. And when I saw *E.T.,* I knew it wasn't really about a boy and an alien but about a boy learning to empathize with others. Most stories that resonate with audiences have a human story at their center.

This may sound to some like basic knowledge, but I rarely see it in the films being made today. And if it is there, it is simply tacked onto a "cool concept" rather than being the reason to tell the story. The best storytellers have used this method over the centuries, from Aesop to Jonathan Swift to Gene Roddenberry to Paddy Chayefsky.

The above quote from Sydney Pollack is about this very idea—your story is not about what happens; it's really about why it happens. Why are you telling this story? That's what your story's about.

Opponents of this method believe that it makes the work trite and preachy. But the purpose of drama is to demonstrate, to dramatize. This means showing that to face your fear is to conquer your fear, as both *Jaws* and *Aliens* demonstrate. This allows the audience to come to conclusions on their own so that they don't feel spoon-fed.

I rarely see a film nowadays that knows what it's about. It is "about" the plot. Or it is "about" the amazing concept. But there is nothing stopping these filmmakers from using a cool concept to tell a story that matters.

If you don't already work this way, it may give your work more emotional and thematic depth to give it a try. If it works, you can thank Paddy Chayefsky.

Posted Tuesday, December 28, 2010

The Strength of the Reluctant Hero

"Courage is not the absence of fear, but rather the judgment that something else is more important than fear."
—*Ambrose Redmoon*

"Courage is resistance to fear, mastery of fear—not absence of fear."
—*Mark Twain*

HOW MANY OF YOU READING THIS are fearless? I mean, you are afraid of nothing, from heights to public speaking to snakes to death. Nothing.

My guess is that we all have something we would rather not do or face. And there are some things we don't even allow ourselves to entertain. For the construction of drama, these fears are fertile ground.

Too often, I see films where the hero is gung-ho for any situation. He is ready with a clever quip, a wink, and a smile with lines such as, "It's go-time," or "Let's do this thing," or "Let's rock and roll." Nothing scares this person.

Sure, sometimes these lines can make an audience cheer with a Pavlovian response, but it is a cheap way to get that cheer. A fearless hero is less of a hero than someone who overcomes fear. It is the facing of these fears that makes one heroic, not the actual deed performed.

The so-called reluctant hero is a hero, while the fearless hero is a cartoon. Ironically, a character who has fear but confronts it will feel more real to an audience, even if that character is actually a cartoon.

Look at *Finding Nemo*. The father, Marlin, is deathly afraid of the ocean and its dangers, but when his son, Nemo, is lost, Marlin faces his fear and conquers it.

In *Aliens,* Ripley is afraid of facing the aliens. She knows how dangerous they are. All of her shipmates were killed—and that was only one alien. I'd be afraid, too. Wouldn't you?

Many of you who have read the work of Joseph Campbell or Chris Vogler know of the idea of the "Refusal of the Call." This is the part of the Hero's Journey that follows the hero's "Call to Adventure."

Lots of people learn these steps and follow them when they create their own stories, but they seldom ask why these steps are there. I believe it's because the steps mirror life. How many times have you been asked to do something or been given an opportunity and have been paralyzed with fear at the prospect? It is always much easier to stay in the world and circumstances you know. It's dangerous out there.

I am reminded of my father wanting to take the training wheels off my bike. I protested and was so frightened that I cried. But my dad knew I could ride without the training wheels and took them off. He steadied me on my bike and held me up so that the bike would not fall. Then I went to look up at him, and he was gone! He was far behind me. I was riding by myself. My father smiled broadly—proud of me. And I was proud of myself. I had been reluctant, but I faced my fear and conquered it.

I'm not saying that I was heroic learning to ride a bike, but the steps and feelings do mirror the mythic steps of the Hero's Journey. I am sure that without too much struggle, you can pull up a similar experience from your own life.

You may have been afraid of a new job or a promotion at your current job. Maybe it was a fear of parenthood. Or maybe it was a new relationship. Or maybe it was leaving a relationship. Maybe you are reluctant to start writing that novel or screenplay. You get the idea.

The reluctant hero is true to life. It is true to how we experience life—we are often reluctant to leave the world we know for the dangerous and unknown.

Creating a reluctant hero makes him or her someone the audience can empathize with. I don't know about you, but I'd rather not find myself in a nest of murderous aliens. What makes Ripley heroic *is* her fear. The fear is what makes the story worth telling. We learn from the story that we might conquer our fears if we confront them.

In *Jaws*, Chief Brody is afraid of the water but must overcome his fear to kill the shark terrorizing his town. His last line in the film is, "You know, I used to hate the water." Just like me on my bike, he faced his fear and defeated it.

Over the weekend, I saw the film *The King's Speech*, a movie about a man with a debilitating stammer who faces and conquers his fear of public speaking. In this story, it makes him an admirable and heroic figure. People clapped at the screening I saw. Like my dad watching me on my bike, the audience was proud of this character's courage. They rooted for him throughout the film. They empathized.

Don't ever forget the power of a reluctant hero; it is a way to draw people into your story. This reluctance makes heroic acts even more heroic and makes heroes more human. It makes your story universal.

POSTED WEDNESDAY, JUNE 18, 2008

THE END: ALL ABOUT ENDINGS

"Begin at the beginning and go on till you come to the end; then stop."
—*Lewis Carroll*

ENDINGS COME UP A LOT when I'm teaching. Some people say that a happy ending is cheap and that life doesn't work out that way. Others feel as if a happy ending is the way to go. And there is, of course, the twist ending. Which one should you choose? You should not choose any of them. Endings should be where your story has been headed the whole time.

I can tell by the way people talk about endings that they think of stories in pieces rather than as a unified whole. Think of a story as a finely tuned machine. Each piece of this machine may be well made in its own right, but its job is to serve the whole.

I can hear that people are thinking of story components as separate from the whole when they say things such as, "The dialogue was good." Or "I liked the characters." Or "There were some good parts."

We teachers talk about story components to make it easier to comprehend, but in truth, all of these components should work in concert to produce a satisfying story.

One type of ending is not inherently better than another; it is all about which ending the story needs to make its point. Endings may be discovered, but they are not decided on.

People tend to fixate on the type of ending that corresponds with their worldview, and they force their stories to have this type of ending.

Greek dramatist Euripides said, "A bad beginning makes a bad ending." And legendary filmmaker Billy Wilder said, "If you have a problem with the third act, the real problem is in the first act."

What both of these storytellers are saying is that a story is a unified whole—one thing informs the other. Everything in a story should be connected.

A story has a proposal, an argument, and a conclusion. Once you make your story's proposal, you are bound to prove or argue that proposal. If your proposal is "There is no honor among thieves," then your ending is the one that best proves this point.

Billy Wilder also said, "Know where you are going." That is because everything in your story should be leading there. Your beginning and your ending are linked. They are tied together by your second act. These parts are one thing, much like the human body. Your body has many parts, but it adds up to one body, each part working in concert with the rest.

So the next time you are trying to work on your ending, ask yourself which ending makes your point. If your ending doesn't work, perhaps it's because you didn't start off in that direction.

POSTED THURSDAY, JANUARY 4, 2007

THE NEW HOLY GRAIL

PEOPLE TELL ME ABOUT HOW GOOD the stories are in games nowadays, but I have never seen this to be true. The games are exciting and the graphics are great, but they do not tell stories. (I can hear some of your knees jerking from here, but hear me out.)

Because video games have many of the elements of a story—characters, settings, and exciting events, for instance—it is easy to be fooled into thinking that you are "in" a story when playing a game. You are not. What you are doing is playing out a scenario.

If the object of the game is to kill the dragon and save the princess, that is a scenario, not a story. Take chess: it has characters and goals very much like a video game. The object is to capture the opposing king without losing your own. There are bishops, knights, and foot soldiers called pawns to help in this task, yet it is never called a story. Why?

I believe we have been tricked by our technology. If chess had been invented as a video game, people would undoubtedly say it had a great interactive story, different every time. Same thing with board games: in Monopoly you can go to jail, buy a house, run a hotel, or own a railroad, but would you say a board game tells a story?

In the old days—the very old days—a hunter might go out and have an adventure while tracking and killing his prey. Upon his return home, he would tell the story of his quest for food. Exactly how his trip went ("First I turned left at the rock...") is not a story, but the retelling of his adventure is.

The term "interactive story" is a misnomer. Interactivity turns a story into a game.

People have been playing games and telling stories for as long as there have been people. (I believe the oldest chess reference comes from Persian literature in 600 A.D.) People go to games for one reason and stories for another. The two forms serve very different functions.

Stories are primarily a way of passing along information from one person to another. Good stories remain essentially the same after many retellings.

Games are a way of challenging ourselves, physically and/or intellectually. A good game varies its scenario and makes us change how we play it.

Each plays its part very well. There is no reason to try to merge them. And pretending that you can fails to acknowledge the specific purpose and power of each.

Part Three:
Movies I Like

Posted Friday, March 27, 2009
Movies I Like: *Paper Moon*

"I know a woman who looks like a bullfrog but that don't mean she's the damn thing's mother."
—*Moses Pray* (Paper Moon)

ANYONE WHO SPEAKS TO ME for more than five minutes knows I think that this time we are living in is the worst time in the history of American film. I am not alone in my assessment. Legendary screenwriter William Goldman says the very same thing. And so does filmmaker Alexander Payne. In fact, Payne dates the demise of American film to the same time I do, around 1982.

This does not mean that there have not been good films since 1982, but it was the last great film year that included classics such as:

- *E.T.: The Extra-Terrestrial,*
- *Tootsie,*
- *The Verdict*
- *Gandhi*

These films were all released in 1982. If just two films of that quality came out this year, I'd be amazed. These movies were all huge hits, and all were very different. There was also more diversity of subject matter back then.

Whenever I get on my soapbox about this, someone always asks me what films I like. I answer with a few names of classic films, and they will (always!) interrupt me and say, "Yeah, but what have you liked lately?" The answer is not much. Some years it's nothing. There was a level of story craftsmanship in older films that is almost nonexistent today—outside of Pixar.

But because people always want to know what I like and why I like it, I've decided to recommend a film every now and then.

Some of you who read this blog are younger and have a problem with older films. The acting styles are different. The color may appear strange or, God forbid, nonexistent. The music cues may seem over the top by today's standards. The special effects may be corny because your eye is used to CGI.

I'm going to ask you to try to look beyond all of that to see the craft underneath. I want you to see the craft that transcends style and taste. I want you to see the quantifiable quality of these films.

I will start with a film I wish I had made: *Paper Moon*.

Released in 1973 and directed by Peter Bogdanovich, this film is one of my all-time favorites. Nothing like it is being made today. It was written by Alvin Sargent, who wrote *Spider-Man 2*. And actress Tatum O'Neal became the youngest person ever to win an Oscar. She still is. When you see the film, you'll know why.

What does the film do well? Everything. The big question is what makes a father: biology, or loving and taking responsibility for a child? You will see that the question of parentage comes up right away in the very first scene, and it never stops. The film never forgets what it's about. Listen to how often it comes up blatantly or in more subtle ways, such as how alike the "father" and child are. Also look for great visual storytelling. See how much is told with pictures and not words—this is first-class screenwriting.

In this film, you care about the characters and what happens to them. Films today don't make you feel as much as they make you think. We seem to have made a collective decision that thinking is better than feeling. But sometimes the emotion of a situation is the truth of a situation.

Nowadays, when I ask people if they liked a current film, they say, "Yeah? It was good? I liked it." They are tentative when they speak. The film may have made them think, but they felt nothing. They are afraid to commit strongly to an opinion for fear of judgment. When *Paper Moon* came out, people liked it. Period. And they weren't afraid to say it. They said, "It's great! You should see it!" They said the same of *Jaws* and *The Godfather*.

Unlike many, many films today, *Paper Moon* does not rely on a gimmick that pulls you out of the film. You will not have to have read the book. You will not have to go to a website to find information on something you didn't understand. You will not have to know that there is a special shot in the film that no one had ever done before. You will simply have a great time, and you will be moved.

Today, filmmakers may make hits, but they almost never make classics.

Posted Friday, October 29, 2010

Movies I Like: Butch Cassidy and the Sundance Kid

WILLIAM GOLDMAN, WHO WROTE THE SCRIPT for *Butch Cassidy and the Sundance Kid,* is one of the most respected screenwriters in the history of the medium. This film is one of the reasons why. It has left an imprint on the "buddy picture" that has not diminished since its 1969 release.

What I love about this movie is that it has a laser focus—it knows what it's about. Goldman knows his theme and drives it home at every opportunity. Sure, the film is fun. The banter between the two lead characters, played by Paul Newman (the salad dressing guy to you young people) and Robert Redford, is clever. The actors have chemistry.

But this film is much deeper than it appears. It says that we cannot run from death. Sooner or later, the world changes, and try as we might, we cannot stop this encroachment any more than we can stop death from coming. It says that, and it's still funny. What more can you ask for?

These two men are notorious bank robbers, and in the very first scene, we see Butch (Paul Newman) casing a bank. Upon seeing that it is heavily fortified, he asks a guard:

BUTCH: What happened to the old bank? It was beautiful.
GUARD: People kept robbing it.
BUTCH: Small price to pay for beauty.

Right off the bat, the world is changing and challenging. These are the first lines spoken.

Not very much later, the next scene in fact, we are introduced to Sundance (Robert Redford). He is in a saloon in the midst of a two-man card game when Butch comes by to collect him. But there is a dispute, and the other card player thinks Sundance has been cheating and says as much. The man, named Macon, also threatens Sundance:

MACON: You can die—no one's immune—you can both die.

It is clear that guns are about to be drawn, and Butch tries to talk his buddy out of shooting it out with the other man. He says to Sundance that he doesn't know how fast Macon is. Then he says:

BUTCH: Well, I'm over the hill—it can happen to you—every day you get older—that's a law.

It is very precise language that gets to the heart of the film—the point of the film. Getting older is a law. It is a law that even these master outlaws cannot break. When most people say that a film had good dialogue, they do not mean something like this—this is great dialogue because it matters.

Goldman never drops the ball on this. At one point, he introduces a brand new invention called a bicycle, which represents the coming future. In fact, Butch, who buys the bike at one point, discards the thing with the line:

BUTCH: The future's all yours, you lousy bicycle.

But the outlaws keep trying to hold onto their past, to the old world. At one point, they rob a train. They have robbed this train before, and the owner of the company isn't happy about it. He hires a "superposse," as the screenplay calls it, to hunt down Butch and Sundance.

This posse is almost superhuman in their ability to track Butch and Sundance over every type of terrain. They never seem to tire. They are relentless. And we never see their faces. They are almost always black silhouettes in the distance. They are death. And you cannot outrun death.

I won't tell you the ending, but it is the only ending there could be to this story. This story may not sound like it would be fun to watch, but it is. It's great. I wish that any film I saw in the theater today had as much to say and could say it with the skill of *Butch Cassidy and the Sundance Kid*.

Most classic films are classics because they are done with much more skill than others, with much more focus and precision. That's a law.

Monday, November 8, 2010

Movies I Like: Shadow of a Doubt

ALFRED HITCHCOCK'S DIRECTING CAREER spanned from 1922 to 1976: 54 years. He started with silent film and saw the advancements of sound (he made the first British talkie), color, and even 3-D within his lifetime. And he was a master of filmmaking almost from the beginning.

Some of his classic films include *Blackmail, The Lodger, Rope, Strangers on a Train, Lifeboat, Dial M for Murder, The Man Who Knew Too Much, Vertigo, North by Northwest, The Birds, Rear Window,* and *Psycho.*

My personal favorite, followed closely by *Rear Window,* is *Shadow of a Doubt,* released in 1943. Not only did Hitchcock direct, but the great Thornton Wilder (author of the classic Pulitzer Prize-winning play *Our Town*) wrote the screenplay. This was Hitchcock's personal favorite, and it is also David Mamet's favorite Hitchcock film.

If you have read any of my previous posts, you'll know I believe that a great story has a focus, a direction. It knows what it's about and what it's trying to say.

In the first act of *Shadow of a Doubt,* we are introduced to a young woman named Charlie, who is tired of her boring town and her boring family. Nothing exciting ever happens. She lives a Norman Rockwell existence.

She wants to break up this monotony and goes to the telegraph office to invite her favorite uncle, also named Charlie, to come visit.

But when she gets to the telegraph office, she finds that a telegram from her uncle saying he's on his way is already there for her. The two Charlies have a special connection.

What the girl Charlie eventually discovers is that her uncle is a notorious murderer on the run. Uncle Charlie is not the kindly, affable man he pretends to be. Now that she knows the truth about her uncle, all Charlie wants is her old boring life back.

This is a Thornton Wilder theme: that life—even a simple, uneventful life—is a wonderful thing that we do not take the time to appreciate. You can see this theme in *Our Town* after one of the characters dies and is able to go back and see/relive moments in her past. She chooses an ordinary day, nothing special, and she is surprised to realize that people don't find each moment of their life precious.

This is the very same theme in *Shadow of a Doubt*. Young Charlie had a good life, and now she wants it back. But it is too late. She knows what she knows and can't return to that life.

This is a deep theme dressed as a common thriller, and it is so much more. As a thriller, it is Hitchcock at his best. And as a piece of art, it is Wilder doing what he did best.

I have to admit that there is a tacked-on love story that I believe the studio wanted—another writer handled that (some things never change)—that is not on par with the rest on the film, but the film is too good to be ruined by this. Hitchcock himself was never happy with the love story.

When I say they don't make movies like they used to, this is what I mean. If I see a thriller now and say it was empty and meaningless, people say to me, "What do you want? It's just a thriller!"

You know what I want? *Shadow of a Doubt*.

Posted Wednesday, November 17, 2010

Movies I Like: Sunset Boulevard

"Grab 'em by the throat and never let 'em go."
—*Billy Wilder, talking about the audience*

THE MAJOR AND THE MINOR, Double Indemnity, The Lost Weekend, Sunset Boulevard, Ace in the Hole, Stalag 17, Sabrina, The Seven Year Itch, Witness for the Prosecution, Some Like It Hot, The Apartment, and *The Fortune Cookie* are just some of the classic films co-written and directed by the great Billy Wilder.

This list does not even include the classics he wrote as a screenwriter before he became a director. You could do worse than studying the work of Wilder, and I could talk about many of his films, but one of his best is *Sunset Boulevard*.

What's so great about it? What isn't?

The film is about a young, struggling Hollywood screenwriter in the 1950s who is in debt and desperately needs a job. Through happenstance, he ends up the kept man of a movie star whose best days during the silent era are behind her.

The film starts with the young screenwriter, Joe Gillis (played by William Holden), floating dead in a swimming pool as his voice-over narrates the scene. He explains how he always wanted a pool but that the price proved to be too high. Then he says he will tell us the story of what really happened here, and the story flashes back to the true beginning of the story.

Here's what's great about this opening. It starts with a great "outer boundary," as I call it. That is, right away the story lets you know what can happen, and will happen, in this story's world. It lets us know the most extreme thing that can happen in this reality.

The classic film *It's a Wonderful Life* begins with angels depicted as pulsating stars in the sky talking to one another. It is a long time before anything else supernatural happens in the film. But when it does happen, the audience has been primed for it and has no problem believing the fantastic.

This is the same trick used in the opening of the film *Raiders of the Lost Ark*. We see the main character in fantastic situations, and so we believe it later. We have been primed.

The other thing these scenes do is whet our appetites for what is to come. We want to know how this fantastic thing links up with the rest of the story.

In the case of *Sunset Boulevard*, we want to know how Joe Gillis ended up dead in a pool. This is a very smart way to open a film. It grabs the audience.

In act one, we see Joe Gillis being hounded by repo men for his car. He spends the first act looking for money and a job so that he can keep his car. While trying to outrun the repo men in a car chase, he ducks into the garage of an old dilapidated mansion. He thinks it is abandoned. It is not.

This is what I call the Land of the Dead. All stories have a point where characters enter the Land of the Dead. These are places where things are in disrepair. Things may be rotting or in decay. Sometimes there is death or the very real possibility of death in these places. Or people may be hurting physically, emotionally, or spiritually. There is often isolation or loneliness. One or all of these things may be present in the Land of the Dead.

Wilder makes sure that this house is a dead place. It feels like a mausoleum. There is death here, as you will see when you watch the film.

It is here that Joe Gillis meets Norma Desmond, the old silent movie star played by the real-life silent movie star Gloria Swanson.

This is a woman who will not let go of the past. She lives in the Land of the Dead.

In stories, the Land of the Dead is no place to live. One may visit to learn the story's lesson, but in order to be healthy, the hero must leave this place.

Because Joe Gillis needs money, he ends up becoming the kept man of this woman. He is her pet. She has money and he has none. Joe feels trapped in this dead place. At one point, the house butler, Max, tells Joe that Norma Desmond is suicidal, and in order to protect her from herself, there are no locks on any of the doors.

This may seem like a detail that doesn't matter, but think about it. Joe feels trapped here and is expressly told that there are no locks. Thematically, it means he can leave whenever he wants.

There is a great scene when Norma throws a New Year's Eve party, and Joe is surprised that by design he is to be the only guest. This is a dead place without life—no guests at a party. Frustrated, Joe leaves the mansion to find a party with life in it, but as he tries to leave, his clothes get caught on the door handle. This is a perfect thing for the story thematically for a man who feels trapped.

This is the story of a man who learns that living as a poor person among the living is better than being wealthy in the Land of the Dead.

There are about a million good things to say about this film, but the main thing is that every element is there to help tell the story. The mansion is not creepy for the sake of being creepy. It has to be a mausoleum. There are no guests at the party not to have an odd scene but to drive home that this is a place without life. What could say that better than a party without guests?

Everything in Wilder's films is there for a reason. No fat.

Posted Monday, August 3, 2009

Movies I Like: It's a Wonderful Life

SOME FILMS ARE RESPECTED and less loved, and some are beloved and less respected. *Citizen Kane,* for instance, is respected but not beloved like *The Wizard of Oz.* A few (very few) are both loved and respected—*Casablanca* is a prime example.

As a rule, films that make us think are respected while those that make us feel are beloved. Film scholars and critics mostly keep the respected films alive. But those films that are beloved are kept alive by the public—a public that cares little about the use of a deep-focus technique or reflections in windows, a public that has never heard the term *mise-en-scène.*

I have great respect for films and filmmakers who make us feel or, God forbid, entertain us. Critics would have us believe that this is an easy task but not a very noble one. As a society, we tend to regard emotions as secondary to intellect.

Scholars and critics dismiss those films that move us in favor of those that bore and confuse us. They would have us believe that any hack can make their point clearly and move people in the process, but that it takes a real genius to make us scratch our heads and wonder what we've just seen.

My argument is that any child could make something that is difficult to understand, but it takes someone with a full command of craft to communicate effectively and move people.

One of my all-time favorite films is one of those films that are beloved rather than respected: *It's a Wonderful Life*. This is an amazing piece of filmmaking, as good as anyone has ever produced. Do not hold it against the film that people actually watch and enjoy it.

What's so great about *It's a Wonderful Life*? Everything. The script is amazing. And although director Frank Capra is known for sappy films, the film also delves into some dark places where most modern films seldom go.

The story is amazingly focused. When it starts, there are voices praying for George Bailey (Jimmy Stewart). Someone says that he needs help and mentions that he never thinks of himself. This is the heart of the film.

In the film, George Bailey is, even as a boy, a person who dreams of traveling the world, but every time he is about to leave his sleepy town, something comes up to stop him. The truth is he is not stuck. He chooses to stay. Why? Because as one of the first sentences in the film states, he never thinks about himself.

Selflessness has been the mark of a hero as long as human beings have told stories. It is this selflessness that keeps George Bailey in this town. It is also George's selflessness that makes him a person liked by everyone in town. (Watch the film carefully and see just how many times George could leave his sleepy town if he just thought of himself before others.)

The villain, Mr. Potter, thinks only of himself and is hated by the townspeople—and the audience. Villains have been selfish as long as there have been stories.

There is even a great scene where George is tempted to cross over to "the dark side." He is offered everything he wants, and all he has to do is think about himself for once in his life. All he has to do is be a little selfish, and he can have everything he wants. But George, good to his core, rejects this deal with the devil.

This story is at once mythical and human. We understand George Bailey's frustration at not getting the things he wants in life because we all feel this frustration. He wants a better house and a better car, and he wants to travel the world. But when he is given the chance to have these things, he turns them down each and every time because that is the nature of heroism: selflessness. We wonder if we could be as strong. We hope that we would be.

Not only is the story worth telling, but it is also well told. The filmmaking is as good as anyone's. People don't pay much attention to Carpra's incredible filmmaking, but this is because they are sucked into the film emotionally.

Watch the scene where George decides to let his brother take a great job rather than stay stuck in their little town. The scene is all played out on Jimmy Stewart's face. You see his whole world crumble. Not many directors would have allowed that huge event to happen in such a small way.

This film is as worthy of study as anything made by John Ford, Orson Welles, Akira Kurosawa, or anyone else. Making people feel is not a lesser form of art than making people think. Communicating clearly is not more easily done than confusing them.

Over the generations since its release, *It's a Wonderful Life* has become a beloved family classic. But it should also be respected as a stunning piece of craftsmanship and art.

Posted Friday, June 5, 2009

Movies I Like: *The Apartment*

"The best director is the one you don't see."
—*Billy Wilder*

SOMEONE ASKED ME TODAY why I like older movies better than new ones. This is not an easy question to answer to everyone's satisfaction, but I will give it a try. I like older movies because they're better.

This is not to say that all old films are great, but they are better on the whole. The level of storycraft in older films is higher. As further proof, I give you another example of a film I like: *The Apartment*.

Anyone who talks to me for about thirty seconds figures out that Billy Wilder is my favorite filmmaker. Wilder understood how to tell a story as well as anyone in cinema ever has.

What makes him so good? No fat. Everything matters. He writes with the steady hand of a master surgeon. He is always advancing plot, character, or theme—sometimes all three.

Wilder once boasted that there was never a phony shot in any of his movies. What he meant was that he never put his camera anywhere where it didn't help to tell the story. He was not a show-off—he was a craftsman and a storyteller.

Just as with his camera shot choices, Wilder also never had a phony scene, sequence, character, or line. Everything matters. Every choice is made in the service of the story. No fat. Nothing phony.

So many modern-day filmmakers are trying so hard to be noticed. The shots are there to be noticed. The characters are there to be noticed. The editing is there to be noticed. It all has the effect of pulling us out of the story rather than pulling us in. All phony. All fat.

Wilder had a highly successful screenwriting career in which he honed his storycraft before becoming a director. The story was always paramount with him. I tell my students that you are not the master of your story but a slave to it. You must do what it needs, not what you want.

On the surface, *The Apartment* is about a man who lets the higher-ups in his office use his apartment to have adulterous affairs and how he falls in love with one of the women. But there is a deeper story about two people who learn to value themselves enough to stop prostituting themselves.

It is a marvel of construction, and the more you learn about story construction, the more you will marvel.

The film was made by a man at the top of his craft. In the hundred-plus years that people have been making movies, few have made one as good as *The Apartment*.

Do yourself a favor and see this film.

Posted Saturday, December 18, 2010

Movies I Like: *Tootsie*

ANYONE WHO HAS READ MY FIRST BOOK, *Invisible Ink*, knows how highly I think of *Tootsie*. It was one of the many standout films—along with *E.T.*, *The Verdict*, and *Gandhi*—that were released in 1982.

I am going to talk here, as I have with other films I like, about how impressed I am with the laser focus of this film. It is a story that aims directly at its thematic target and hits a bull's-eye.

I won't take up time here breaking down the entire film, but the first act is so well constructed that there is much to learn from it.

Tootsie was co-written by Larry Gelbart, who in his early career was one of the legendary writers of the Sid Caesar shows *Caesar's Hour* and *Your Show of Shows* in the 1950s. Sid Caesar's writing team included Carl Reiner, Mel Brooks, Woody Allen, and Neil Simon. Heavyweights. Gelbart later went on to create the classic *M*A*S*H* television show in the 1970s.

If you don't know the film *Tootsie*, it stars Dustin Hoffman as an out-of-work actor and acting teacher who, desperate to get a part on a soap opera, pretends to be a woman.

Sydney Pollack, who was a brilliant director and actor, directed the film. Pollack did not want the job until he figured out the film's armature (theme): wearing a dress could make Dustin's character a better man.

I know that Pollack always worked hard to find an opening image that had thematic meaning in his films. The very first shot in *Tootsie* is a long pan shot of a makeup table. We see fake teeth, wigs, and powders, and we end on an actor applying makeup. We don't know it yet, but this is Dustin's character, Michael Dorsey.

We see Michael apply a false mustache. He smiles, proud of his work. The glue unsticks, and the mustache lifts off his face. This is not a small thing. For plot reasons, we want to know he has some knowledge of stage makeup because later he must become another person.

There is also a thematic component here—the mask will come off.

Nothing is random in this act. The next thing you see is Michael Dorsey teaching students. We start to get the idea that he is an actor who knows what he's doing. This becomes very important.

Then we see Michael in an audition. In the audition, he reads lines with a male gum-chewing stage manager. As a response to Michael's line that someone is coming and to put some clothes on, the stage manager reads his line flatly: "I'm a woman. Not Felicia's mother and not Kevin's wife."

Right away, we have a man pretending to be a woman. This is solid construction. It may look simple, but it is hard to do well. And you might think an audience would see something so obvious, but they don't. But they do get a sense that the story has a direction and is not just random lines and scenes.

Michael is told that he's not right for the part—they need someone older, they say.

Next we see Michael in another audition playing the part of a young boy. He is now told that they are looking for someone younger.

In the next audition, Michael is told that he's too tall. He says that he can be shorter. He pleads with them, telling them he can be whatever size they need. They then say that they are looking for somebody different. And he answers that he can be different.

In frustration, they tell him that they are looking for somebody else. Michael has no answer.

What's great about this series of auditions is that we get both thematic and plot information. Plotwise, we know that it is hard for Michael to get work. Theme-wise, we see that he would be willing to change anything about himself to get a part. In fact, he does become "somebody different" to land a part.

We now see him teaching again, and he tells his students that they have to be truthful in the parts they play. I'm paraphrasing, but this is essentially what he says.

Michael then reads from cards as he performs lines from a play for yet another audition. The play seems to be about how you shouldn't do some things for money. This is thematic because when Michael gets the part on the soap opera, he ends up hurting people he doesn't mean to—all because he wanted money.

Next, Michael is teaching again. In this scene, he tells his students that they should not play a part that isn't in them; they must become the characters they play.

This is also thematic. When Michael pretends to be a woman, he must be true to that experience. He begins to see life through the eyes of a woman. This is how "wearing a dress makes him a better man."

Later, Michael is rehearsing for a play, and in the scene, he is dying. He is asked by the director to stand up and move center stage as he dies. This doesn't ring true to Michael, and he refuses. This is also thematically relevant because this is all about Michael being true to the part. If it isn't truthful, he won't do it.

This makes it hard for Michael to find work because he is seen as difficult to work with.

For the sake of space, I will not break down every scene. But some of the plot points we are told in this first act are that Michael's roommate, Jeff, played by Bill Murray, is a playwright, and they need money to put on Jeff's play. We also see at Michael's birthday party that Michael is a bit of a womanizer. He lies to women.

So it is established that Michael Dorsey tells the truth when he's acting, but in life, he can be a little dishonest.

There is a classic scene, also in the first act, where Michael Dorsey agues with his agent (played by Sydney Pollack, the director of *Tootsie*) about not getting him work. In this scene, we hear Michael argue that he must always be truthful to the character he is playing, even if that character is a tomato.

I will let you find the rest of the thematic Easter eggs in the first act of this film. But I will say that this is a film made with fine precision. This kind of craftsmanship is as rare as the dodo bird in films made today.

By the end of this beautifully conceived and executed first act, we find out that our character is a skilled actor who believes strongly that he must tell the truth while acting. We also find that he is not so honest in his life, particularly in regard to women. And we know that Michael Dorsey needs money. He needs a job.

The stage is set. When Michael Dorsey puts on the dress and makeup and becomes his alter ego, Dorothy Michaels, we believe it. We know he has the acting and makeup skills to pull it off.

We also know that Michael has a lesson to learn: he must become a better man.

And we know that when Michael becomes Dorothy, he has no choice but to see the world through the eyes of a woman because he has to become the character. He has to be true to the character. He cannot lie when he's acting. This commitment to character is what forces Michael to change.

If you want to see storytellers working at the top of their craft, watch *Tootsie*. Take the time to really study the film, and it will make you a better writer.

Posted Monday, April 13, 2009

Movies I Like: *12 Angry Men*

"I happen to think that the singular evil of our time is prejudice. It is from this evil that all other evils grow and multiply. In almost everything I've written there is a thread of this: a man's seemingly palpable need to dislike someone other than himself."
—*Rod Serling, Los Angeles Times,* 1967

I HAD A STUDENT ONCE who would always ask me what films I liked. He was confused as to why I almost never liked anything new. I did what I always do, and I talked about craft and the lack of craft in the writers and directors making films today.

So the student asked me to name films I liked and why I thought they were so much better. I listed a few and then asked him if he had ever seen *12 Angry Men*. He hadn't. I told him that it was well written, well directed, entertaining, engaging, and smart. That is a combination that is almost never seen anymore. I said to this student, "I just want to go to the theater and see *12 Angry Men*." I meant, of course, that I want to see its equivalent, a movie that is both meaningful and entertaining, both emotional and important.

This student, unlike most, took it upon himself to watch *12 Angry Men*. The next time I saw him, he said to me, "I just want to go to the theater and see *12 Angry Men*."

This, like *Paper Moon*, is one of those films that I wish I'd made. One of these days, if I study really hard, maybe I can write something as well as Reginald Rose wrote—*12 Angry Men*.

I've said it before, but those guys knew what they were doing back then. They felt a social responsibility to tell stories that were relevant and felt a responsibility to engage an audience.

My pet theory, which I cannot back up in any way, is that the writers who fought in World War II felt a real responsibility to their friends who had died on the field. They saw just how inhumane human beings could be to one another, and they wanted to remind us to be as good as we could be, and to be as fair and compassionate as we could be.

The message is all over my hero Rod Serling's work.

But at the same time, these artists strove to teach, not preach. Drama is a way of getting an intellectual idea across on an emotional level.

12 Angry Men is a story that says each of our voices matters—that because of our personalities and experiences, we can all bring something to the table. It is a story that says we all have value.

It also shows how our prejudices can blind us and how foolish it is to stick to them despite all evidence to the contrary.

12 Angry Men is a masterpiece, plain and simple. It is a lean drama stripped to its essence, all the fat trimmed off.

Do yourself a favor and look past your own prejudices of style, or what you think of black and white film, or old acting styles, and see what's underneath all of that. Treat yourself to the rare experience of both feeling and thinking as you watch a film.

Posted Wednesday, July 21, 2010

Movies I Like: *Norma Rae*

THERE ARE MANY FILMS THAT I LOVE, but there are only a few I wish I had made. One of those films is *Paper Moon*. And then there are a few films where the pure craftsmanship brings me to the verge of tears. These films make me shake my head in admiration and disbelief at their excellence. *Norma Rae* is one of those films.

I told someone once that it was one of my favorite films, and she was surprised because the film has a female protagonist. That doesn't matter to me at all. If the character is a human being truthfully portrayed, that's all I need. Race, gender, religion, or any other circumstance of the character makes little difference. Is the story truthfully told? That's what matters.

Norma Rae is truthfully told. Directed by Martin Ritt and written by Harriet Frank Jr. and Irving Ravetch, it stars Sally Field, who plays the part flawlessly. She won an Academy Award, in fact.

The film was released in 1979. Sally Field plays Norma Rae, a woman from a small southern town who struggles to organize a labor union in the textile factory where she works.

It doesn't sound exciting, I know, but it is real human drama that is engaging and entertaining. It is not boring because it deals with "important" issues. In fact, one of the most beautiful things about the film is that Norma's personal story is the story. The story is really about how she grows as a person. She learns that she has a value beyond her sexual relationships with men.

The storytellers understood that in order to make viewers care about the issues, they would have to use drama to do it. What I mean when I say "drama" is that they knew to tell a human story full of emotion.

As I pointed out to someone recently, the ancient Greeks, who invented the dramatic form we use, knew that it was based on emotion, not puzzles or philosophy. That's why the symbols they (and we) use for drama are the masks of Comedy and Tragedy and not of someone thinking. The Greeks believed that co-suffering was good for the soul, that weeping for the characters on the stage was a way to gain a particular kind of knowledge. The Greeks are well known for their philosophers, but it's clear that they felt drama served another function.

Norma Rae uses emotion to make its point. It tells the story of a person standing up against a corrupt system and suffering the consequences. It challenges us to stand up against our personal Goliath even though we are small.

One of the very first things you see Norma Rae do in the film is an example of its beautiful craftsmanship. Remember, the film is about her trying to get a union for her fellow workers. Well, the film starts with Norma Rae helping someone.

I will often say that a great film is focused, and this is what I mean. Nothing is random. This film knows what it's about from the very beginning and stays on track.

Most of the storycraft will be invisible to you, but I assure you, it is a meticulously made film. They just hid most of the work so well that you can't see it. But you can't make a film like *Norma Rae* by accident.

I wish I had written this movie, but if I had done so in our current film climate, it would more than likely be sent back by my agent because nothing blows up and there is no twist ending. And my agent would be right not to send it out because the studios don't make films like this anymore. It's a cryin' shame.

Posted Thursday, September 18, 2008

Bad Shark, Good Movie: Thoughts on *Jaws* and Other Things

BACK IN THE DAYS BEFORE CGI, my roommate was a special effects makeup artist. At that time, I had a few friends in this field. There was an ongoing argument that I would have with my creature-making friends about Yoda and E.T., back when both of these characters were made of rubber. They were really just sophisticated puppets.

My roommate's view was that both E.T. and Yoda were poorly sculpted. It bothered him that Yoda looked like puppet. Now, he may have been correct, but it doesn't matter.

Jaws was released in 1975, and the shark looked like a big rubber piece of crap. This did not prevent the film from becoming the *first* summer blockbuster, one of the highest grossing films of all time and a bona fide classic.

How did this happen? Spielberg and editor Dede Allen kept the shark off-camera as much as possible (partly because the thing didn't work). This allowed the audience to use their imaginations. Not a bad strategy.

They also told a good story and created characters we cared about. This is a novel idea in today's Hollywood, but it used to be standard practice. Creating compelling characters and putting them in a story for an audience to be invested in produces the illusion of life better than any computer imagery ever could.

Yes, the audience could see that Yoda was a puppet, but they were so interested in this unusual character that they allowed themselves to be "fooled" into believing he was a living, breathing being.

E.T. was another example of a puppet (albeit a sophisticated puppet) that people believed was a creature with feelings, dreams, and motivations. I saw the film in 1982, and I don't remember a single person in the audience saying that the puppet was poorly sculpted. People cried when E.T. "died" and cheered when he was revived.

With all due respect to Carlo Rambaldi, who built E.T., the first step in making E.T. live was writing the script. Melissa Mathison made the alien come alive on the page. She constructed a story that made us sympathize with a fictional alien when he was left behind on a planet not his own. Her words made us both happy and sad when E.T. went back home.

Today we could arguably make a "better looking" E.T., but he would not be any more believable. In recent years, we have spent a lot of effort trying to make creatures look more real. Maybe they do look more real, but they don't feel more real. No one cries when they die.

Our job as storytellers is to make characters as real as possible so that people can suspend disbelief. Our job is to make it so bits of rubber or bits of digital information can live in the minds of the audience. When I was a kid, there were few television stars as big as Miss Piggy and Kermit the Frog. By no standards do these characters look realistic. They do, however, live, as far as the audience is concerned.

For thousands of years, people have imbued puppets with emotion and feeling. The puppets can be crude or sophisticated; it makes little difference. If the story is relevant and well told, people will believe even a sock puppet can talk.

My hope is that Hollywood will once again concentrate on story and storytelling instead of empty spectacle. Spectacle is not what pulls us into the film experience. No, it is character and story that do that. If filmmakers get that right, we will fear a rubber shark, cry for a dead puppet alien, or even worry about a digital fish lost in the big ocean.

No matter how much better technology gets, it will not improve on good story-craft. Make your characters live on the page and they will live on the screen.

Posted Tuesday, May 15, 2007

A Genius

"I like Keaton's [films]. But Chaplin is the best of 'em all."
—*Howard Hawks*

CHARLIE CHAPLIN WAS A GENIUS. I know I'm not the first one to say this, but people tend to take him for granted. We think of his Little Tramp character as too cutesy. We are too sophisticated nowadays to laugh at something so corny. He doesn't look funny to us with his Hitler mustache, bowler hat, and baggy pants. But once upon a time, Chaplin made the whole world laugh and sometimes made them cry—very often, both at the same time.

Like Alfred Hitchcock, Chaplin could play his audience's emotions like a violin. If you call yourself a student of film and don't make yourself familiar with his work, you are doing yourself a disservice. His films are the best film school you could ever attend. Some of the best filmmakers in the history of the medium have been influenced by his work: Woody Allen, Chuck Jones, David Lean, Walt Disney, and Martin Scorsese are just a few.

What made Chaplin so great? It was his uncanny ability to put a dash of pathos in his comedy. It was his ability to communicate visually. Chaplin was great at everything.

He was a master at the art of pantomime. It is my firm belief (as it was Chaplin's) that pantomime is older than spoken language and communicates more clearly. Even dogs who want to be petted pantomime the action to communicate their needs. It is an ancient form of communication that, when done well, speaks to us more deeply than spoken words.

If you want to tell stories on film, then visual storytelling is your stock-in-trade. You would do yourself a big favor by sitting down in front of the television and going to Chaplin University.

My favorite Chaplin films are *The Kid, Gold Rush, The Circus,* and *City Lights*. When you watch these films, it will help if you remember that the gags you are seeing were brand-new at the time. Chaplin was the first to think them up and execute them. You may be familiar with some of the gags because you've seen them used in a Chuck Jones cartoon (i.e., Bugs Bunny, Daffy Duck, etc.). Or you may be familiar with some of them out of context and are likely to shrug them off because you have seen a clip used in a cheesy commercial to sell you a mattress on Labor Day.

Try to work through that secondhand familiarity and put yourself in the audience's place, seeing these things for the first time. If you can allow yourself to do that, you will not only learn something about your craft, but there's a good chance you will laugh your ass off.

Posted Thursday, July 22, 2010

Movies I Like: Planet of the Apes

"Overall theme leads to characters then on to plot."
—*Rod Serling*

IT WOULD TAKE ONLY A CASUAL GLANCE at my writings to deduce that I'm a huge Rod Serling fan. Frankly, I wouldn't be surprised if people are tired of reading about it. I'll try to lay off. Right after this…

When I was a very young boy, my father spoke with wonder and excitement about a film he'd seen called *Planet of the Apes*. He spoke about it with such joy. It is possible that my love of film started at that moment.

I have to admit, when I did see the film, I was just as impressed as my father had been.

It wasn't until years later that I would know the film was co-written by Rod Serling—or even who Rod Serling was.

Serling was the creator of an early television classic called *The Twilight Zone*, a show known for strange happenings and twist endings. But for me, what shines through his work is his love of humanity coupled with his profound disappointment that we can be a cruel, self-destructive, and greedy species.

This can be seen even in his work that precedes *The Twilight Zone* when he was writing for the live television dramas of the early 1950s. His work spills over with humanity.

For better or worse, because of *The Twilight Zone,* Rod Serling has become known as the twist ending guy.

People who are not practitioners of something are often impressed with the obvious. People who don't act, for instance, think that crying on demand is good acting. Or that being able to do accents or memorize lines is good acting. Trained actors know differently. A lot of work that people don't notice as easily goes into great acting.

In writing, the twist ending is one of the things that people are very impressed with. But what is often overlooked is that Serling's endings were linked to the story's theme—the reason to tell the story.

Serling's screenplay for the original *Planet of the Apes* is very much like a feature-length *Twilight Zone.* (By the way, I used to tell people that *Planet of the Apes* was just a long *Twilight Zone,* that it had all the same structure, but people said I was crazy. Then some guy cut a short version of the film and made it into a *Twilight Zone* episode, and people were surprised at how well it worked.)

OK, back to the monkey movie. *Planet of the Apes* is a film where the twist blew people away. In the opening of the film, an astronaut on a starship tapes a log. In it, he talks about how long he's been away from Earth and that much time must have passed on Earth because he and his fellow astronauts have been traveling at light speed. Then he says, "I wonder if Man, that marvel of the universe, that glorious paradox who has sent me to the unknown…still makes war against his brother and lets his neighbor's children starve."

This is the theme that the entire film explores: are human beings essentially warlike, self-destructive creatures? The story never loses track of this.

So Taylor, the astronaut, and his fellow travelers crash-land on an unknown planet. At one point, as they walk through a desert looking for food and such, they have this exchange:

> LANDON (heatedly): You thought life on Earth was meaningless. You despised people. So what did you do? You ran away.

> TAYLOR: No, not quite, Landon. I'm a bit of a seeker myself. But my dreams are a lot emptier than yours. (pause) I can't get rid of the idea that somewhere in the Universe there must be a creature superior to man.

There it is again. Human beings are not so great.

Later, intelligent apes with the power of speech capture Taylor. On this planet, human beings are primitive brutes who cannot speak (Taylor's throat was injured during his capture and he cannot talk). One of the apes, Dr. Zaius, talks to another in front of Taylor's cage:

> ZAIUS: Men are a nuisance. They outgrow their own food supply in the forest and migrate to our green belts and ravage our crops. The sooner they're exterminated, the better.

Here it is again. Humans are self-destructive—but this time out of the mouth of someone other than Taylor. Now Taylor finds himself trying to argue on the side of humanity.

This point of view is consistently stated throughout the film.

At the end of the film, Taylor escapes the apes only to discover the Statue of Liberty buried in the sand. He has been on Earth the entire time. Humans have destroyed Earth. This "twist" is right in line with what the film has been saying the whole time. We brought about our own destruction by way of a nuclear war.

If the three acts can be defined as proposal, argument, and conclusion, then we can look at Taylor's speech as he records his log at the beginning of the film as a proposal. The second act is the argument when the opening statement or proposal is debated. So the conclusion of the film is proof-positive of what the film has been saying all along.

This is not just a trick—it is storycraft.

Serling's stories are timeless, and they matter. In the 1960s, when he wrote the film, the Cold War was raging, and people felt that any minute, the world might end by our own hands.

Today, although it is still a possibility, we are slightly less worried about the nuclear threat and more about an environmental one. But it doesn't matter what method of possible destruction is referenced, only that we may be the ones ultimately responsible.

Great stories are never just timely; they are also timeless.

Rod Serling was so much more than a writer of twist endings. He was an artist and a craftsman.

AFTERWORD

THAT'S ALL I HAVE TO SAY for now. If I continue to blog and people care to read it, maybe I will do another volume.

I have been lucky so far that people care to read what I have to say and tell me that they learn from it. I do not take this for granted. Like many writers, I have toiled for years without access to an audience, and it is a privilege to now have one.

If you are one of those toiling writers without an audience, I hope I can help you a little in reaching your goal of becoming better known. And if you are a writer with some success, I hope you found something within these pages that helped you see things in a slightly different light.

As we all know, writing is something that takes time to master—we are forever students of this craft.

THE END

GREAT READS FROM TALKING DRUM, LLC

Invisible Ink **by Brian McDonald** Invisible Ink teaches the essential elements of the best storytelling from award-winning writer/director/producer Brian McDonald.

The Golden Theme **by Brian McDonald** The Golden Theme is the study of writing's essential commonality by award-winning writer/director/producer Brian McDonald.

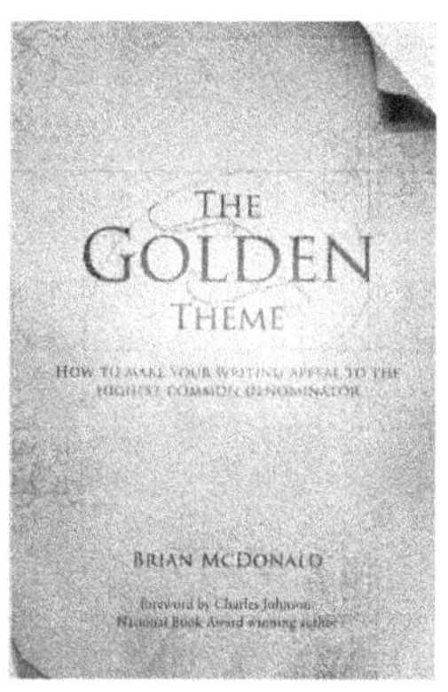

www.ingramcontent.com/pod-product-compliance
Lightning Source LLC
Chambersburg PA
CBHW021404090426
42742CB00009B/1006

* 9 7 8 0 9 9 8 5 3 4 4 4 2 *